The Scandinavian Garden

Karl-Dietrich Bühler

FRANCES LINCOLN

For Kristina, Martin and Violette

Frances Lincoln Limited
4 Torriano Mews
Torriano Avenue
London NW5 2RZ

The Scandinavian Garden
Copyright © Frances Lincoln Limited 2000
Original text copyright © Karl-Dietrich Bühler & Milena Matteini 2000
English language translation © John Margetts 2000
Photographs copyright © Karl-Dietrich Bühler 2000
Redrawn garden plans copyright © Frances Lincoln 2000
First Frances Lincoln edition 2000

British Library Cataloguing in Publication Data
A catalogue record for this book is available from the British Library
ISBN 0 7112 1506 5
9 8 7 6 5 4 3 2 1
Printed & bound in Singapore

HALF TITLE Annual beds in Karen Blixen's garden at Rungstedlund, Denmark
TITLE Sven-Ingvar Andersson's topiary garden near Södra Sandby, Sweden
OPPOSITE Ornamental ironwork with clematis and blue glass ball in
Tommy Nordström's garden at Simrishamn, Sweden

Contents

Introduction 6
by Milena Matteini

A Voyage 9

Landscape & Woodland 12

Seaside & Lakeshore 86

Town & Village 124

A Walk through the Scandinavian Garden 168
by Milena Matteini

Bibliography 189

The Gardens & their Designers 189

Index 189

Acknowledgments 192

Introduction

Scandinavia is the name we use to denote the four nations of Denmark, Sweden, Finland and Norway. Sparsely inhabited by people who are lovers of nature and ruled by governments with a strong tradition of social engagement, they are all too easily dismissed in our collective imagination as countries with endless summer nights and the briefest of winter days. They do share characteristics as a result of their geographical location and the passage of a history that has seen them bound together, but there are also many differences.

Denmark, today the smallest and the most populous of the four, stretched as far as Norway and the south of Sweden until the beginning of the nineteenth century. Sweden included a part of modern-day Finland, while Carelia, Finland's most easterly region, shared a border with Russia. Therefore it is not surprising that, at the same latitude, the gardens of Norway and Denmark have more characteristics in common, than do Norway and Finland.

Southern Denmark maintained close ties with the European continent. In 1562 King Christian III and Queen Dorothea had Koldinghus built according to the principles of the Italian Renaissance garden, and it was thanks to their contacts that the art of garden design began to spread throughout the kingdom. The publication in 1647 of the treatise *De horticoltura danica* by Hans Raszmusson Block shows that the garden was long-established in Danish culture, and there is continuing awareness of its traditional forms; elsewhere garden history has been more recent in origin (Finland) or is being rediscovered (Norway), or both (Sweden).

Sweden presents many of the landscape elements that are characteristic of the Scandinavian countries as a whole. In its southern part, the landscapes are gently undulating, almost flat, and accented by the tall, thin silhouettes of modern windmills, as in Denmark, where almost everywhere agriculture has created a fabric of carefully cultivated plots of land. The noble families who still inhabit the many fortified houses scattered principally across the region of Skåne are the custodians of the garden in its most refined state. These gardens, which date for the most part from the 1600s and 1700s, were laid out on formal lines within the area enclosed by the moat that surrounded the house, while the park or outer area drew its inspiration from the model of the English landscape garden.

As we advance north and west through Scandinavia, the countryside becomes harsher, culminating in the spectacular grandeur of Norway where mountains plunging sheer into the sea alternate with dense coniferous woods. The Gulf Stream washes the western coastline and relieves the harsh climatic conditions.

In Norway recent studies show that, from medieval times, here as in other parts of Europe Cistercian monks had pioneered the tradition of the monastic garden, rich in fruit-bearing trees and aromatic herbs. Large gardens of more classic form were few in number and were subsequently destroyed. One exception is Rosendal Barony, which still retains the design created by the Dutch gardeners engaged in 1660 by the first Lutheran bishop of Bergen.

Moving north and eastwards, a succession of woods, lakes and clearings heralds the arrival of the Finnish countryside where water is such a dominant feature that many villages bear names associated with its presence, such as *Joki* (river), *Jarvi* (lake), and *Saari* (island). Here the year is marked not so much by the passage of the months as by the change from winter to summer. The cold season has very few hours of light, and the complete covering of snow and ice alters our sensory perceptions; both earth and sky are of a whiteness that seems to stretch to infinity. It may seem absurd to say so, but the impression of limitless space and the immense silence is the same as that which we might experience in the desert or the African savannah. The summer season, while brief, is both warm and colourful. The sun remains on the horizon for many hours and within the Arctic circle it never sets. The length of the sun's rays can make the water of the lakes seem almost white – sometimes with delicate shades of pink – and creates a special atmosphere which has been a source of inspiration for many artists. The light is tranquil and a little melancholy, so different from the exuberance of the Mediterranean world. Between these two seasons comes the magical moment of reawakening in late spring: the snow and ice melt and the countryside is once more delineated by water and somehow seems to shrink as the land takes repossession of its boundaries.

In this the most easterly of the Scandinavian countries, cut off yet further from the rest of the Continent by a language with no Indo-European roots, gardens in the usual sense of the term are an exception. Within the cloisters of the Greek Orthodox churches, the tradition of the walled garden (*Hortus conclusus*), arrived from Russia. There was no landed nobility desiring to vaunt its power by building gardens. In a country so marked by the presence of untamed nature, and by a farming tradition that embodies the struggle for survival, gardens were considered to be a useless luxury. In gardening terms, it may be more meaningful to speak of nature 'managed' as a transitional step between the house and its surrounding countryside; or perhaps of the 'temporary garden' – a reference to those brief moments of summer when bulbs and biennials explode into flower, only to close down again within the space of a few months. Even staples such as ivy and box cannot survive the climatic conditions here. Yew and privet take their place in the more protected areas, and farther north beech, fir and ash (*Sorbus* sp.) predominate before the tundra takes over. In the forest, where the sun's rays barely penetrate, different types of birch alternate with the conifer and ash, while the undergrowth is rich in bilberries and raspberries growing amidst the moss which clings to smooth granite rocks.

This brief, and somewhat incomplete, look at the background to the Scandinavian garden concludes with a dedication – to the private gardens of today. Those chosen represent most faithfully, in the judgement of Karl-Dietrich Bühler, the spirit of Scandinavia in all its aspects. Often small, sometimes very small, in size, they place emphasis on detail and on the pleasure to be derived from their use as a continuation of the house, but at the same time are respectful of the surrounding environment. A profoundly poetic world lies waiting to be discovered.

Milena Matteini, Genoa, 1999

OPPOSITE Clouds and reflections in a mountain lake on the way to Bergen.

A Voyage

Many years ago I photographed my son Martin as a small, fair-haired boy cheekily chasing six geese who were fleeing from him: the geese belonged to Ella, our neighbour, and they were visiting our 'garden' – so-called, for it still had to be made into one. My thoughts turned to the miraculous journey through Sweden of the tiny boy, Nils Holgersson, from Selma Lagerlöf's *Tom Thumb*; what he sees and experiences on his journey with the wild geese is an exciting story with its lively description of landscapes, animals, people and historical events and it is still well worth reading. Our garden in Hedeberga, Skåne, is situated in the parish of Tomelilla, which means 'small thumb', and it provides the starting point for my journey to gardens in Scandinavia, which is also a flight of the imagination.

Like Nils Holgersson and his wild geese, we explore Skåne in southern Sweden. Our tour takes us past meadows and fields, which Nils sees from the air as a large check quilt, made up of big and small squares of material. In a fairy-tale grove near Lund we come to Sven-Ingvar Andersson's gigantic birds that years before started out as small hawthorn chickens. We bid them farewell and continue through the landscape of Småland, a region of poor soil that Selma Lagerlöf called 'a tall house with fir trees on its roof, a broad stairway with three huge steps leading to the landscape of Blekinge'. In the middle of a forest near Värnamo, the painter Sten Dunér presides in his magical kingdom, a Swedish idyll but also a place where the 'blue flower' of Romanticism of the German writer-philosopher Novalis flourishes. Further north in Näs (some way from Tranås), we reach a small lake with Helena Emanuelsson's flower bed in pastel colours along the shore. Then we take off towards the west, to a garden on the sea coast in Långedrag, and on to Göteborg and Norway, where in the country south of Oslo six new geese are waiting. This time they are not real but are made of light wood: Egil Gabrielsen's poetic windmill geese in front of his ochre-yellow house.

At Lidingö the hillside sculpture garden of Carl Milles (1875–1955) is well worth seeing, and close by at Stockholm the evening ferry boat departs for Finland. Our sunset voyage through the countless islands of the Skärgården is exceptionally beautiful. In Helsinki I photograph a garden by Gretel Hemgård against the backdrop of architect Pekka Salminen's studio, and west of Helsinki, there is Hvitträsk with its famous lakeside houses and gardens designed by Saarinen, Lindgren and Gesellius. I take a motor boat eastwards to the Island of Mölandet, where the landscape architect Tom Simons has uncovered the natural beauty of a rocky plateau with wonderful mosses and lichens among pine trees. Then on to the north, west of Tampare, in search of Alvar Aalto, in the forest of Noormarkku. His Villa Mairea is a classic example of modernity, with its garden integrated into the forest setting. And finally, to the Island of Seurasari, north of Tampare, where Aalto's holiday home in the forest of Muuratsalo is a discreet, poetic piece of

architecture. Returning to Sweden when the heather is in flower, I photograph the pinewood setting of Per Friberg's two transparent holiday homes in Ljunghusen, Skanör-Falsterbo, trees and clear architecture again blending happily. Kaare and Torborg Fröhlich's wooden house near Bergen is another exemplary piece of architecture harmonizing with its setting, the panoramic windows encompassing their nature garden.

The Scandinavian garden is interwoven with architecture, literature, painting and music. Where the harsh winter climate limits plants, fantasy flourishes. Here in the north a fine feeling has developed for form, colour and atmosphere. Goethe said that each living thing forms an 'atmosphere' around itself, and this is so whether it is small or great. Trees, especially, create atmosphere – in photographic terms this is symbolized by the contrast of light and shade – and bird song, the humming of bees or children's happy voices all create their own.

If Karen Blixen's Rungstedlund is a key to Danish literature and garden culture, Edvard Grieg's Troldhaugen near Bergen is a key to Norwegian music and atmosphere. At his 'hill of the

BELOW *Haväng*, land where sea and meadows meet, by a frozen river delta on the Baltic coast.
OPPOSITE Harvest fields, forest and lake in Finland.

trolls'. Grieg composed music which is full of the sounds of the west Norway that he loved: 'The whole atmosphere of Bergen… the smell at the German Quay (*Tyskebryggen*) still fills me with enthusiasm, indeed there is even codfish in my music', he said.

Music opens up the heart to the possibility of 'renewal', or new beginnings, yearned for by so many people today. Music, landscape and garden design have in common themes, rhythm and also duration: music is fleeting and so are flowers, scent and light. The great Danish landscape architect Carl Theodor Sørensen (1899–1979) called his garden work of art in Herning, Jutland, 'The Musical Garden'; it is a sequence of geometrical forms and spaces with hedges in harmony. He developed strong geometrical forms in his gardens, such as that for his daughter Sonja Poll, or in the garden colony of Naerum.

A theme which glances across the pages of this book is the garden as a place of contentment for children. C. Th. Sørensen, a designer with a pronounced social concern, had a special feeling for children. Noticing that they particularly liked being on building sites and playing where there is an element of risk, one of his initiatives in the fifties and sixties was to provide large areas in Copenhagen, supervised by trained teachers, where surplus planks, boxes and junk such as old cars were made available for play. Called '*skrammellegplads*' ('scrap/junk-playgrounds'), these were places where children could hammer away, build things, take things apart and develop creativity. At the beginning of the seventies I went to Copenhagen to make a photographic report of one such playground in the suburb of Emdrup, where children were holding bread dough in the fire on long poles, and it was during this visit that I got to know this wonderful 'inventor' of adventure playgrounds, whose creations also brought greatness to garden art.

Karl-Dietrich Bühler

Hedeberga, July 1999

In a dream, Nils flies over the windswept landscapes where clouds fly fast, riding a goose…

Landscape & Woodland

Fairy-tale Grove in Box & Hawthorn

ABOVE The morning sun shines through the silver willows and spreads light over the small white house under the tall trees. Patches of light dance across the round fairy-tale privet sculptures. BELOW A photograph taken in the 1970s when Sven-Ingvar Andersson's hawthorn 'chickens' were still small and the blue cushions of lavender sent out their attractive scent. OPPOSITE Twenty years later the chickens have changed into gigantic birds and the lavender has given way to the magic rings of box.

Sven-Ingvar Andersson's remarkable gardens lie hidden behind high hawthorn hedges near Lund, on the road to Södra Sandby, Approaching the white-painted, black-beamed 'Marnas hus' sheltered by tall willows, the visitor is greeted by a collection of strange, round, green shapes. In the light that plays over them you can make out a gathering of giant tortoises, which the master has sculpted out of privet and trained with a combination of infinite patience and garden shears.

Around the corner, to the right of the entrance, a broad vista opens up, framed by tall hawthorn hedges in part formed into green pilasters. A fantastic scene of a flock of gigantic hawthorn birds is scattered among roundels and cushions of box along this fine grove, which Andersson modestly calls his 'chicken run' (a name presumably dating back to a time when these fabulous creatures were smaller and daintier). The ground beneath the stately, long-necked birds is strewn with sky-blue forget-me-not flowers in spring and later with abundant bright mauve-pink globes of the long-stemmed *Allium hollandicum* and violet, red and white columbines that mingle with the white flowers of wild garlic (*A. ursinum*) to produce a joyful scene. The severely trimmed hawthorn hedges and huge sculptures provide a fascinating contrast to the flowers in and among the box circles. Each flower stands out against the white gravel or green hedging, its character defined by its colour and shape, as on a theatre stage.

Further gardens, in sunshine and shade, also enclosed by hawthorn hedging, lie behind the bird grove. In Beate's garden (it belonged to Sven-Ingvar's then small daughter), there used to be the scent of primulas, tulips and daffodils. Now, in the shade of the hawthorn hedges that have grown tall, lilies-of-the-valley (*Convallaria majalis*) are in flower and a green carpet of ivy spreads peace and quiet. The so-called flower garden used to be a small kingdom of lilies, where today the common

Södra Sandby, Sweden

ABOVE The end of the chicken run. A shining pale wooden sculpture stands out at the end of the hawthorn grove. Within a box ring are *Allium hollandicum*'s globe-like seed boxes that come into effect after the glow of its mauve-pink colouring, and to the right there is the delicate scent of the white flowers of soapwort (*Saponaria officinalis*).

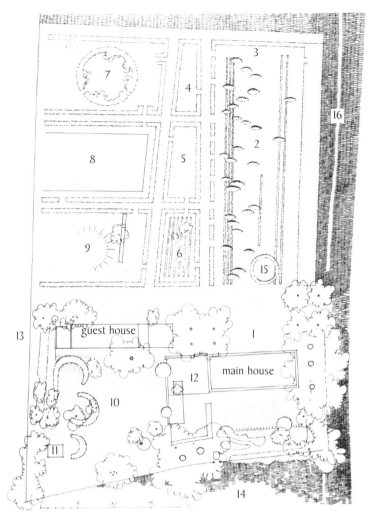

1 turtle walk
2 'chicken run'
3 'Diana', a wooden sculpture
4 Beata's garden
5 sun garden
6 flower garden
7 compost yard within a mixed hedge circle
8 kitchen garden
9 sitting & barbecue area

10 arcs of privet in part of former orchard
11 summer house
12 terrace (former stable yard)
13 field
14 meadow
15 privet circle (now removed)
16 double hawthorn hedge

LEFT Along a mossy path edge sits a small blue-painted ceramic form. It was made by Gustav Kraitz, a well-known ceramicist. The creeping plant is ivy-leaved toadflax (*Cymbalaria muralis*), which one finds here and there on old walls, particularly in churchyards. RIGHT Sven-Ingvar Andersson's 'Diana', a figure created from driftwood. It stands on the north-eastern side of the kingdom of the giant birds in front of a dark hawthorn hedge, enlivening the shady corner and giving pleasure to visitors.

turkscap lily (*Lilium martagon*) with its small racemes of flowers dominates and the pink-coloured climbing rose called 'Fragezeichen' ('Question Mark') flowers luxuriantly on a trellis. In the sun garden, shielded from the wind between green walls, one can sunbathe without being disturbed. The compost lies in a circle made up of various bushes. In winter there are the shining red stems of red-barked dogwood (*Cornus alba* var. 'Sibirica'), then the pre-spring flowers of the cornelian cherry (*Cornus mas*) and in summer and autumn the decorative berries of the spindle tree (*Euonymus europaeus*), the snowberry (*Symphoricarpos albus*) and the Oregon grape (*Mahonia aquifolium*). Here charm and usefulness are united in a circle of the seasons.

To the north-east, the gently falling terrain lies 3 metres (10 feet) lower than at the top of the slope, but the green walls are cut to give the impression of being all the same height. Andersson planted these hedgerows over thirty years ago, on what was then a ploughed-up field. He decided to cut them so that at the highest point of the terrain they are only one metre (3 feet) high, but rise to 4 metres (13 feet) near the road. The hawthorn, which has been established in the Skåne countryside for centuries and is of a pagan beauty and strength, is repeated through Andersson's garden like a musical theme. The composer of this symphony in green who, for many years before his retirement, was Professor of Garden and Landscape Design at the Copenhagen Academy of Fine Arts, has had a number of commissions on the international stage. His best-known projects are the Karlsplatz in Vienna, the square at La Défense in Paris and the Museumplein park in Amsterdam.

His own garden here at Södra Sandby, he took over from his parents, who at the time had a fairly large farm, more than forty years ago. Sven-Ingvar inherited his love of plants from his mother and as a five-year-old boy had his own little garden enclosed by a border of stones. Down the years 'Marnas hus' has remained his playground as well as his garden for experimentation, using a minimum of materials but extracting a maximum number of detailed variations.

Behind the house is a pleasant terrace and an old orchard where simple privet has been transformed into arcs for sheltered sitting places. At the far end of the garden a black summer house almost disappears in the dense, green foliage. Inside, it is sky-blue with a white floor and white window frames. An airship candelabra is suspended from the blue firmament of the ceiling, and as it swings gently to and fro, the visitor's imagination is inspired to fly off into a world of poetry.

ABOVE At the upper end of the old orchard, where the privet hedges form rooms and green sculptures, there is an unobtrusive, black summer house with tall, arched windows, open like a gazebo to the view. A climbing hydrangea (*H. petiolaris*) reaches up to the roof and when its white flowers come out, they transform the dark architecture of this small, enchanting building.

RIGHT Inside, Sven-Ingvar Andersson's 'cloud-cuckoo' summer house is full of atmosphere and harmonious colour. The large windows with their rounded arches came from the former Hirschsprung tobacco factory in Copenhagen. The poetic candelabra is a dried branch which hovers from a chain and wire amidst the 'clouds' and the dark blue 'firmament' of the ceiling.

Fields, Flax & Clipped Hedgerows

Three giant hawthorn balls by the side of the road leading to the small village of Flade announce the home of sculptor Erik Heide on the Island of Mors, which is linked to Jutland by a bridge. Beyond the entrance an exciting garden awaits the eager visitor. It lies on a south-facing slope, with its greater part divided by hedges into elongated spaces on different levels. On the top of the hill is a meadow of wild flowers and grasses. At the bottom of the slope near the road, great yew hedges crenellated like a medieval town wall and scaled by climbing roses frame a small garden filled with roses and lavender.

Rising up the slope is a series of three gardens, each on a slightly different level and each surrounded by beech hedges. The first level has a garden of flowering shrubs and ornamental artichokes where a carpet of leaves is stippled red with wild strawberries. The next garden up contains standard redcurrant and gooseberry bushes and a small greenhouse, and the hedges above that conceal a mixture of summer flowers and herbs.

The hedges, planted more than twenty years ago following the plans of the landscape architect Sven Hansen, structure the garden, lending it a stylish appearance; their architecture corresponds to the white walls of the house under its steep, black roof and the light-coloured garden walls at the side of the house. They provide a quiet architectural background for the multitude of plants with colours and forms that are seen at their best in these separate areas. Erik Heide keeps the beech hedges perfectly trimmed at exactly 1.2 metres (4 feet) high and 30 centimetres (12 inches) wide. They are cut at the beginning of June and a second time in August. This precise hedge architecture more than proves its worth, as its foliage turns a flaming reddish-brown in autumn and is still beautiful in winter.

Each garden level is a world in itself, and has its own shapes, colours and scents created by Erik's wife Bente, who chooses the plants. Scented sweet peas (*Lathyrus odoratus*), mallows,

Flade by Limfjord, north-west Denmark

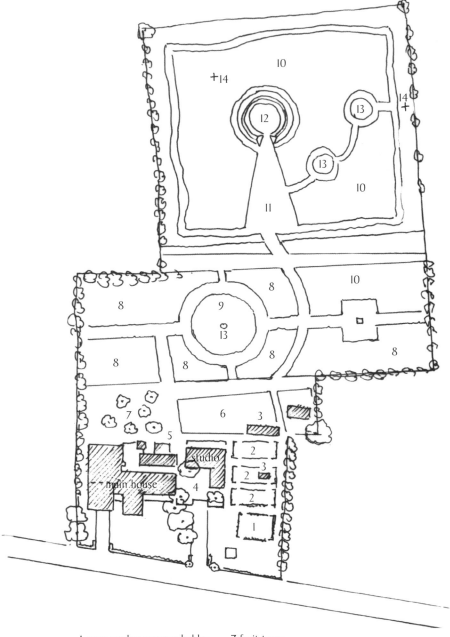

1 rose garden surrounded by beech and yew hedges
2 three gardens enclosed by beech hedges
3 greenhouse
4 courtyard
5 henhouse
6 hawthorn hedge enclosing former kitchen garden, now wild grass
7 fruit trees
8 young oak woodland
9 mown area enclosed by hawthorn hedge
10 wild meadow
11 mown grass paths
12 fire place
13 circles of flax or cornflowers
14 cast iron crosses

RIGHT The entrance to the garden is marked by three large balls of hawthorn. Here and there the visitor comes across Erik Heide's sculptures in the garden. This one, '*Sofias sol*', the sun of Sofia, consists of two granite stelae and a perforated, rust-brown cast-iron shape 'hovering' in between. In the background the tall ash trees that mark part of the boundary of the garden run along the road.

BELOW In the evening light the lines of the hedges on the slope melt together with the golden fields and the cloudy sky of Mors beyond. Three longish spaces are surrounded by beech hedges. The highest level is planted with herbs and summer flowers. White sweetpea (*Lathyrus odoratus*) is visible climbing up a red iron support and there are dill and strawberries. The next level down is reserved for currant bushes and gooseberries. The third garden has white flowers of delphiniums, ornamental artichokes and more perennials and bushes flowering throughout the summer. At the bottom the crenellated yew hedges can be seen, where roses and lavender flower.

ABOVE Heide has christened the cast-iron work of art at the upper end of the hedge garden 'Grekiska Fötter' ('Greek Feet'). The inspiration for it came to him on a beach in Greece.
BELOW One of the oldest sculptures made of grey granite: a small girl waiting patiently at the bottom of the hedge garden.

the white clouds of *Gypsophila paniculata*, white larkspur (*Consolida*), hydrangeas and the delicate yellow of flowering dill flourish under the protection of the hedges. Some of the entrances to these hedge gardens are guarded by Heide's oldest sculptures, sparingly chiselled out of stone.

Between the house and studio is a small courtyard with white walls and a white staircase flanked by pots of lilac-blue horned violet (*Viola cornuta*). This leads to a raised sitting area with a massive stone table. This bright courtyard has an air of the south with its large vases that contain an olive tree, blue African lilies (*Agapanthus*) and oleanders, awakening memories of the Mediterranean. Erik Heide's dark cast-iron sculptures form a strong contrast to the white walls.

Going through the courtyard you come to the chicken run, though it looks more like an aviary for rare birds. Its low white walls, which are stepped to correspond with the rise of the slope, and its black wooden beams that support the wire netting make a fine architectural feature.

Our walk takes us higher up the slope past Heide's rust-brown and reddish iron sculptures, which stand out among the green of the trees and bushes. We are now in the middle section of the sloping terrain, which on the plan looks like a longish rectangle. In this meadow, which climbs on up, Erik Heide has planted in recent years a lot of small oak trees, the common oak (*Quercus robur*), which in time will form a small wood. Paths have been mown into the meadow which widen out into a round area and a smaller square. The green mown circle is surrounded by a medium-sized hawthorn hedge (it is the white-flowering whitethorn, also known as 'may', but which flowers here in June) and in its centre shimmers flowering flax like a blue eye.

We climb further up the slope and reach an open landscape, a meadow with waving grasses, which up here have a more noble effect than down below. There are wild flowers here as well. The path to the knoll gets narrower and narrower, thereby

RIGHT ABOVE In the top garden herbs and exquisite vegetables for the kitchen flourish together with flowers. Behind strawberries on the left are the white flowers of mallow (*Lavatera trimestris*) and on the iron trellis sweet pea (*Lathryus odoratus*). A spreading cloud of *Gypsophila elegans* mixes with the delicate yellow of dill (*Anethum graveolens*). To the right there is parsley (*Petroselinum crispum*) with its tightly curled leaves, borage (*Borago officinalis*), French beans and lastly the bluish leaves of leeks. RIGHT The transparency and reflected greenery of the greenhouse's glass panes allow it to blend in harmoniously. Bente uses it as a cold greenhouse for plants with white blossoms, such as arum lilies (*Zantedeschia*), clematis, carnations and fuchsias as well as lilac-coloured greenhouse roses, which are used as cut flowers.

increasing the upward perspective and dividing this sea of grasses, which in the evening light change to the most delicate filigree patterns. Right at the top there is a round place, a spacious crater for making a fire. Archaeologists have found traces of graves from the Prehistoric and Bronze Ages here, but nowadays this magic spot is the favourite place of the Heide family for parties with friends and for meditating when the sun is setting on the Limfjord. Another path leads away from the fireplace to a blue island of flax shining amidst the bright yellowish-brown of the long grass. Next morning, in the dew, the fallen stars of flowers shimmer pale blue on the brown earth.

The grasses and wild flowers are mown only to make a path or reveal a blue island of flax or cornflowers. Heide leaves everything else here to nature, in direct contrast to the hedged gardens down below, which require a good deal of work. Here at the hill-top, this can be forgotten amidst the tall grasses waving in the wind. Erik Heide's cast-iron cross stands close by, like a mediator between the ancient myths of a saga-rich past and our own age. Instead of a wide horizontal arm, the vertical of the cross bears a small angled slab. It is a cross without severity, which all the more easily guides our thoughts upwards. Farther down, on the slope of the meadow, a tall cross of St Andrew stands half-submerged in the grass. Both these sculptured crosses remind us that Erik Heide's art has shaped the interiors of many churches in his Danish homeland. His works, mostly of granite and cast iron, can be found in public places throughout Denmark.

The path takes us close to the high cross sculpture from where we can look down on green or gold landscape and across to the horizon. Erik Heide, with his white flowing beard, looks like an Old Testament prophet gazing out over the Promised Land. Here and there on the edge of a sea of corn we can glimpse the waving arms of the simply designed white windmills, which, as symbols of our own age, form a not unhappy union with the landscape of the Island of Mors.

LEFT ABOVE & BELOW Erik Heide's cast-iron cross with its tilted slab makes a sympathetic bond with the distant windmills. Lower down the hill he has wrested two round, flowering islands from nature. Here, a small island of cornflowers nestles amidst the gold of the grasses. To keep the earth loose and fruitful, Heide also grows tasty potatoes on his islands in the sea of grasses which before their harvest also provide beautiful flowers.

RIGHT The mown path to the knoll narrows as it rises, so appearing longer than it really is. Grasses and flowers stand out as beautiful filigree against the mown grass. The artist's touch is also revealed in the shaping of this meadow. Right at the top he has moulded a spacious crater, a place for making a fire.

Rock Outcrop with Flowers and Pines

Patches of early morning sun illuminate a moss-covered rise of rock in a hilly suburb of Oslo, bordered by birches and rowans. My sense of anticipation grows for a garden that I had heard so much about as now I glimpse it up among the high pine trees. Broad wooden steps, cleverly anchored in the rock, climb all the way up to the house through the gentle vegetation. On the left I pass the ample, airy pink of meadow rue (*Thalictrum aquilegiifolium*), toned down by the shade, and am drawn on up by the scarlet red of a rhododendron in the sun by the house. Grethe Li gives me the name of this hybrid, 'Fireglow', and leads me around this beautiful house that she planned and built with her husband Olav in 1976. This achievement is all the more impressive since the Lis are neither architects nor builders by profession, but school teachers, now retired. However, both of them taught applied art, among their other subjects.

The comfortable house was positioned in such a way that rock blasting could be avoided; it was only necessary to carry out a small amount for the cellar entrance, the water supply, the sewers and at one point for the steps leading up to the house. Otherwise the cliff was preserved in its original beauty. Before any blasting was done, all the trees round about were given protective padding. On the morning of my visit sirens howl; there is a muffled thundering in the air and I think of war – but this war is against nature. It comes from further blasting in the neighbourhood. Perhaps, to take advantage of the short Nordic summer, someone is making space for a stylish sun terrace with a fine panoramic view. But view of what, and in which direction, if the mountain round about has been mutilated and too many trees felled? The Lis have campaigned in vain locally for buildings to be integrated with the natural surroundings and for the restraint in blasting that they themselves demonstrated in an exemplary manner. However, the landscape is being relentlessly urbanized, especially down in the valley, where petrol stations, supermarkets and industry eat into the countryside.

The Lis filled cracks and and cavities on the rocky site, which measures some 700 square metres (7500 square feet), with

ABOVE & BELOW The house is alone but not isolated from neighbouring properties. Here, behind the house, is a seating area on a wooden platform. In front of it, water has gathered in a cavity in the stone and the nearby pine trees are mirrored in it. One can sit and contemplate this watery eye that changes in the light. The Lis have planted a geranium (*G. macrorrhizum*) in an earth-filled pocket in the mossy rock.

Lørenskog, Oslo

ABOVE Solid wooden steps and walkways facilitate getting around the outside of the house and about the mountain slope with its sunny glades. An annual shamrock (*Oxalis corniculata* var. *atropurpurea*) grows in blood-red veins through gaps in the stone and here and there are jolly yellow and orange islands of alpine poppies (*Papaver alpinum*). To the right, in the foreground are pink and white *Saxifraga umbrosa*.

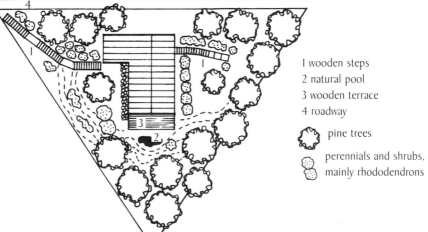

1 wooden steps
2 natural pool
3 wooden terrace
4 roadway

pine trees

perennials and shrubs, mainly rhododendrons

27

stones from the area and a lot of earth. Moss and a creeping variety of stonecrop (*Sedum*) now grows over everything, and the boundaries between the rock and the imported earth and stones have blurred. Farther down there is a small, damp gulley with densely green, wild vegetation such as bilberries, ferns, woodland grasses and dogwood (*Cornus suecica*) with its white flowers with their dark centres, and later on scarlet berries. Grethe Li has planted flowering islands in niches in the stone.

The main flowering period in this mountain garden is from May to mid-June, when rhododendrons and peonies flower and from July until early August when they are followed by divers lilies. There is hawkweed (*Hieracium villosum*), a greenish-white hairy plant with yellow flower heads in panicles, the airy pink and white saxifrage (*Saxifraga umbrosa*) and *Saxifraga paniculata*, with its more powerful, white cup-shaped flowers in panicles. There are greyish-blue cushions and pink flowers of Cheddar pink (*Dianthus gratianopolitanus*). In July the dwarf alpine *Rhododendron hirsutum* has clusters of tubular rose-pink blossoms that flower with the white common turkscap (*Lilium martagon* var. *album*). Grethe, who taught Norwegian and history, is interested not only in botany but in the history of the plants in her garden and mentions the common bearberry (*Arctostaphylos uva-ursi*), a dwarf, evergreen, circumpolar alpine shrub that creeps along the rock here and is successfully used in natural medicine for kidney and urinary complaints.

These two former teachers, who now live so closely involved with nature, are setting us a clear example with their comfortable, self-built house that is so well integrated with the rock cliffs, the surrounding pines and their garden of wild and cultivated flowering plants.

LEFT: TOP The bluish-green leaves of *Hieracium villosum*: hawkweeds are an extremely variable group of plants.
CENTRE *Rhododendron hirsutum*.
BOTTOM *Cornus suecica* and bilberry.

RIGHT Cavities in the rock face were filled with local stones and a good quantity of earth. The result has been the rapid spread of creeping plants such as this annual shamrock, *Oxalis corniculata* var. *atropurpurea* and self-seeders such as the alpine poppy, *Papaver alpinum*.

ABOVE When we first bought the plot of land a rectangular garden was laid out with beech hedges on the outside and box hedges on the inside, which are also effective in the winter. At the back the garden proper begins under elms and ash trees.
BELOW When I see my garden again in the summer for the first time, it seems to have been abandoned for years, but the globes of the dandelions bid me welcome again.

Trees, Banks, Wild Planting & Water

Gardens and landscapes represent memories. I remember the violets of my grandmother Katharina, the bleeding hearts and the scent of lilac in her garden in the small Hessian town of Oberursel, and I remember the undulating countryside of the Taunus hills with their beautiful woods and fields and old homely inns. But the noisy, humming city of Frankfurt am Main spread and became too close for me. After years of wandering, first in the south and then in the north, I found a plot of land with a small house south-east of Skåne, right in the countryside, with old elms and ash trees and a church spire on the horizon, some 20 kilometres (12 miles) from the sea and endless beaches, between the small, picturesque harbour towns of Simrishamn and Ystad. Here, twenty years ago, in the heart of the gently undulating landscape of Österlen, with its extensive apple plantations and nature parks, its ancient Viking Age stones arranged as outline shapes of boats and enchanted castles, I started an adventure with my own garden. But first of all it had to be turned into one! A design had to be worked out for this narrow plot of half an acre (1700 square metres).

The low, white, hundred-year-old house stands in the corner of the site and forms an inner courtyard with a garden wall. The first step was to spread dark grey gravel, which turns black in the rain, in front of the house. This matches the dark grey roof which is a favourite place for moss to settle. Then a Japanese pagoda tree (*Sophora japonica*) was planted in the courtyard close to the house. It is an elegant tree that grows quite slowly in these climes but is hardy enough in its protected position. It is similar to the American false acacia, but waits until August to produce its creamy white flowers and retains its fine leaves a month longer.

I wanted a lot of box, which, whether one likes it or not, is part of the rural atmosphere here. A large clump of box now

Tomelilla, Sweden

RIGHT Predominantly white flowers contrast with grey gravel: in the foreground are bush roses, in front of the wall oxeye daisies under Swiss willow (*Salix helvetica*). Behind is a yew and the rose 'Golden Showers' by the front door.

gives emphasis to the door of the house close to the old bucket-well. I was able to buy as much box as I wanted from a cemetery which was selling off its box hedges cheaply, because it was too time-consuming to trim them. The evergreen hedge, hardened in many winters of growing at gravesides in the local climate, went on thriving in my secular little garden in front of the house without any problems. This garden is a large square, 9 by 9 metres (30 by 30 feet), surrounded on three sides by a beech hedge and divided after the local rural manner into four beds, each divided by box. The entrance to this small garden is marked by two long posts with hops, which grow high up into the branches of an old mirabelle plum tree. I removed the lower leaves from a blackthorn bush and shaped it with shears, then placed a silver glass ball in its black, prickly branches. It spreads light in a dark corner by the box square, shining and sparkling depending on where the sun is and enlivening the garden even on dull days. The four paths along the beds also consist of gravel. This quiet square, framed by box and set off by the beech hedge, is full of the scent of herbs but also, to my annoyance, of the presence of dandelions. Their profusion following my periods of absence and, growing in the heavy clay, their impossibly long tap-roots, drive me almost to distraction.

About two-thirds of the garden is situated behind the house. On this long strip there were a number of old elms, which with one exception have all now died, and ash trees, which continue to influence the atmosphere of the garden. Besides the trees it was the prospect of the hilly fields and the distant white church spire that made me fall in love with this plot of land. But the garden here consisted only of lawn, with a few small, stiff conifers and a straight path of concrete paving stones by the side of the lawn, which emphasized the narrowness of the plot's proportions. The garden needed a complete reshaping. It required hard work, but that is enjoyable and keeps one fit.

During that first summer I received a visit from a Dutch friend, Dick Huigens, a landscape architect from Zeist, and his family. Dick presented me with some sketches made with a few quick pencil strokes and I was delighted with them. They showed banks of earth flowing across the small landscape, dividing it up and enclosing spaces. The following spring I used an excavator and set about reproducing the broad outlines of Dick's drawings, improvising according to the particular effects I wanted or where the ground was interrupted by large stones. First I dug out a hole at the end of the garden for a pond and used the excavated earth for a hillock, but extra earth had to be bought in for this. The bank nearest the house curves to the left, holding in the end of the ample lawn and guiding the view between the trees to the varied landscape of fields. It opens up to the right, to form a round hollow that continues as a bank of roses and ends close to the pond.

I had noticed beautiful, large, roundish stones lying about close to local farms and now collected them using the excavator I'd hired. Of special interest were the so-called 'Johnnies', the ones that were covered with moss, which I used for a dry-stone wall along the boundary of the garden and for the paved round hollow. Here they were piled on top of each other to form a kind of grotto, a sheltered sitting area, like the ones you can still see

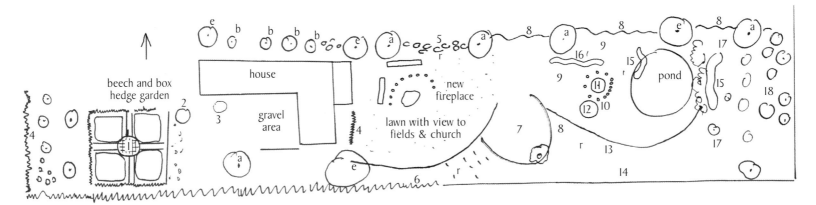

1 Tuscan vase	7 paved 'grotto' with pine tree	13 large stones	18 willow & elder
2 old mirabelle plum tree	8 earth banks covered with ivy	14 *Gleditsia* tree	
3 *Sophora japonica*	9 sand garden	15 old oak trunk, now in two	a = ash trees
4 privet hedges	10 Violette's play place	pieces	b = birch trees
5 low stone wall at field edge	11 young oak with birch trunks	16 box snake	e = where the elms stood
6 ferns	12 Canadian willow	17 bamboo	r = bush roses & rose hedging

ABOVE Beyond the curve of the old mirabelle plum tree we can see the shining grey roof of my house. In the centre of the box garden where the paths cross there is a small square area laid out with Dutch brick, in the centre of which stands a fine terracotta jar from Tuscany. 'Schneewittchen' ('Snow White') roses used to fit in with the dark background, but they were killed off by a severe winter. Now their flowers are present only on a bush variety ('Iceberg'), and bloom together with caryopteris, a small shrub with shiny silver-grey undersides to its leaves and tiny blue flowers that last well into the autumn.

LEFT White foxglove has only arrived in recent years in my box hedge area. Today I would not be without the tall, elegant, white racemes, which for a while give emphasis to the vertical line in this low garden, bowing and swaying with a fine elegance in the wind. Their little bells are dancing in the wind before ever the new 'Snow White' awakens. Happily, they self-seed.

ABOVE A glass ball in the branches of sea buckthorn (*Hippophäe rhamnoides*) and spider webs, when the summer is coming to its end. This shrub had for many years shown where the sandy realm begins, but it grew ever more bent with care and finally had to make way for a large globe of box.

in old farm gardens today. In this refuge the trees with their annual rings and the stones with their rounded shapes polished by the glaciers are the markers of time. I desired to have still more nature and each time when I returned from a journey through Österlen to take pictures, I was impressed by the grasses on the beach, the carpet of flowers on the rocks, and the jungle of ferns in the woods.

Walks along the seashore inspired me to make a sand garden between the pond and the bank of roses, where sea buckthorn, grasses and the dune Scotch rose (*Rosa pimpinellifolia*) with its red hips that change to black would dominate the picture. I would have liked to use fine white sand from the seashore, but that of course was not possible and two lorry loads of finely riddled horticultural sand were delivered and spread over an area of about 100 square metres (1000 square feet). It had first been laid out with hard core for drainage and to separate the sand from the bare earth. I planted some grasses, such as blue oat grass (*Helictotrichon sempervirens*) and blue fescue (*Festuca glauca*) in the sand, as well as thyme and creeping stonecrop and mugwort (*Artemisia stelleriana*), a white hairy perennial. This plant looked very good against a grey piece of wood from the seashore next to forget-me-nots planted on tufa, but rabbits like it as a special delicacy and it has disappeared. The vertical gems are tall ornamental grasses, such as maiden grass (*Miscanthus sinensis* 'Gracillimus') and fishpole bamboo (*Phyllostachys aurea*), a bamboo with gold-green foliage. But the crowning glory is the delicate silver coyote willow (*Salix exigua*), especially when the steel-blue flower heads of the globe thistle (*Echinops ritro*) stretch up into its delicate silvery shining foliage. This Canadian tree is said, not surprisingly, to put up with temperatures, as low as -30°C. In winter, which here is rarely as cold as that, a protective sleeve is placed around its trunk to keep off the hungry rabbits.

The sand garden and pond with its water lilies stand next to each other. The sand covers up the edge of the black plastic

LEFT In my garden, almost at the end of the world, ideas were to blossom and bear fruit; it was to become a field for experiment for the imagination, an open-air photographic studio with fleeting scenes that come and go.
RIGHT The sand garden with a bank and low wall of stones on the left, curving towards the landscape. In the foreground: *Spartina pectinata* 'Aureomarginata', yew (*Taxus baccata*), pink-flowering *Geranium endressii*, the blue globes of *Echinops ritro*; left background: *Helianthus salicifolius* and, last, a *Miscanthus sinensis* .

ABOVE & RIGHT ABOVE On one of these excursions with my camera I had noticed on the edge of a coppice in a shallow bog the bizarre rump of an oak tree; it was just the sort of background I wanted for the pond I was planning. I agreed a price with the owner of the land, an artful farmer, and paid a bottle of aqua vitae, firewater, in exchange for the ancient, fabulous monster from the roadside. Then, with the help of a friendly neighbour, the heavy oak sculpture, which weighed one and a half tons and meant so much to me for my pond, was to the great amazement of the villagers brought some 10 kilometres (6 miles) home. And that is where it lies, but now after some years split into two pieces, one for each side of the pond: part-beast and part-trunk, and looking as if it has always been here.

LEFT I wanted still more nature in the garden, and each time I journeyed through Österlen to take pictures I was impressed by the wild plants I found along the roadsides. Here, tall ferns mingle with alchemilla and white roses.

RIGHT BELOW The pink flowers of Chinese rhubarb (*Rheum palmatum*) that used to flower beyond the pond but after a particularly hard winter did not return. But shortly I shall have another go, since its big leaves give an exotic air to the pond.

RIGHT A blue glass globe swims on the pond where the marsh plant mare's tail (*Hippuris vulgaris*) has spread, and which occasionally has to be kept in check. In the background in the jungle of bamboo and willow, the yellow of *Iris pseudacorus* and the white of *Rodgersia aesculifolia* shine out.

sheeting that was used in the making of the pond, which has steeper sides closer to the moor bed and the oak sculpture. There the black sheeting is covered with felled wood, blocks of peat and stones so that everything makes a natural impression. In the pond itself the lesser bulrush (*Typha angustifolia*) with its brown flower spikes and water plantain (*Alisma*) predominate, and in the moor bed marsh ledum (*L. palustre*) and the noble *Rhododendron yakushimanum*, with a gold coating under its leaves, its white blossoms and delicate pink buds. Bamboos and white willows (*Salix alba*) form the background. Where the bank is steeper, a mountain willow shrub (*Salix hastata* 'Wehrhahnii') does good service.

The boundaries of the garden are kept by a mixed hedge of beech, hawthorn, bird cherry (*Prunus padus*) and snowberry (*Symphoricarpos*), which makes a harmonious transition to the rural surroundings. The dandelions also help to achieve this as they invade the garden from the fields with their parachutes. We use the fresh young leaves in the kitchen for salads or omelettes. We cut the 'lawn', which consists largely of dandelion, with the mower and keep it short, just like proper grass. On the banks the tough yellow flowers are kept in check

ABOVE Violette's play place with lengths of silver birch trunk, the tiny 'umbrella' oak and the Canadian silver willow behind.
OPPOSITE The fireplace that comemorates the last of the old elms, with a sky-blue semi-circle of log seats. The garden is above all a place for friends to come for parties and where children can find a playground.

by lady's mantle (*Alchemilla mollis*) with its strong rhizomes and robust leaves that give good ground cover. This useful and beautiful perennial (which is easily separated into fresh plants), has grey-green leaves and greenish-yellow, veil-like cymes of blossoms. It goes well with all the other colours and covers almost the whole of the bank along the lawn, providing a picture of peace and harmony.

Wild ginger (*Asarum europaeum*) is successful in defending its terrain against the dandelions. It forms thick growths and is a good seeder. In the deep shade, ivy and periwinkle (*Vinca minor*) with its blue flowers cover the ground and grow over the big stones. My favourite among the various bush roses that do well here in the clay soil is 'Louise Odier'. Its heady scent and old-pink, camellia-shaped blossoms continue well into autumn, and it deserves the biggest area.

Twenty years have passed by and there have been many changes. The century-old elm behind the house which gave refreshing shade in summer has had to be felled. Like many of these giant trees, a characteristic feature of the Österlen countryside, it died of incurable elm disease. But there is now more sunlight in the garden behind the house, to the benefit of the rose hill, which is brightened by the shining, young golden-yellow leaves of *Gleditsia* 'Sunburst'. The ash trees of Nordic myth are still there, their feather-like leaves rustling in the wind.

Their gracious arched branches sink down over the sanded area and in the half-shade an evergreen wave of box washes up to a round area of sand which is bordered by blocks of birch wood which provide seating. In the middle there is a small oak tree with its crown like an open umbrella. Beneath this tree the red points of wild strawberries and the larger ones of begonias are visible. Here, close to the Canadian silver willow and tall miscanthus grass, is the tiny kingdom of our youngest daughter, Violette. The oak seedling had sown itself in the moor bed and was tranferred to this spot when the playground for Violette was made; her elder brother Martin helped to lay it out. A row of smaller birch blocks of differing height is grouped here, marking the entrance to the play garden and ending in front of the silver willow. For her birthday Violette was also given a few pots of houseleeks (*Sempervivum*) with their rosettes and some ornamental cabbages.

The trunk of the felled elm was cut down the middle. One half serves as a table for barbecue parties, the other as a sculpture for children to climb over. With all the wood that I got from the tree I had the idea of sacrificing some of the lawn for a hearth, of dedicating this spot in the garden to the magic of fire. Smaller blocks of wood from the elm's branches have been set up in a half circle, marking where it once cast its shade on the lawn. They invite visitors to sit around the fire, warming themselves. Each of these elm seats is painted light blue. Seen from a distance, the painted surfaces appear as hovering greyish-blue circles or ellipses, and so the old elm tree continues to live on in some other form.

Sky & Heath

Where pine forest meets heathland, and the view stretches towards a silver strip of sea, two almost transparent wood and glass houses shelter beneath the pine trees, blending with their natural surroundings. With the evening sun and the sea behind us, we can clearly see from a distance their simple clarity.

The house on the left stands out, its roof visible as a bluish-green horizontal line, which extends right over the glass façade. The copper strip of roof edge, despite its firm delineation, seems to float in the air and harmonize with the blue-green and reddish-brown of the pine trees, so playing a role in the poetry of the architecture. The short, vertical lines of the building's frame graphically divide up its long glass frontage, and a terrace, outlined by the lower, dark, horizontal base line of the building, seems to hover lightly above the ground.

The smaller house on the right is half-hidden behind a denser group of pine trees but the windows, veiled in white curtaining, stand out more strongly than the transparent main house in this light from the west. The space between the houses is clearly defined, yet the distance is so calculated that they form a dialogue with each other.

The architect Per Friberg built the larger house on the left here in Ljunghusen, on the peninsula of Skanör-Falsterbo, south of Malmö, for his family in 1960. Its construction, which could not be simpler, consists of a wooden floor that hovers on concrete pillars a metre (3 feet) above ground level. A flat roof of black-tarred roofing felt covers one single large space measuring 31.5 by 13.8 feet (9.6 by 4.2 metres), with walls of glass on three sides, and also forms a protective collar over the outer wooden platform below.

The house is built with wooden beams and a pine-wood wall on its northerly side. This wood is rough and is painted with black creosote on the outside; on the inside, it is planed but not treated. On this rear wall there are built-in cupboards, beds that can be folded away and kitchen fittings.

A few years later the smaller second house, measuring 23.6 by 13.8 feet (7.2 by 4.2 metres), was constructed in the same

ABOVE The larger, transparent house, with its blue copper strip that protects the roof edge and also brings the structure to life. BELOW Wild heather (*Calluna vulgaris*) stretches in a purple haze across the low-lying heath towards the sea. RIGHT Framed by rowan, honeysuckle, an oak sapling and pines, the platform between the houses is a magical place to linger on beautiful summer evenings.

Ljunghusen, Skanör-Falsterbo, Sweden

way but subdivided into three bedrooms: one room for Per and his wife, one for their two sons and one for their two small daughters. In this way there was a house where the children could be put to bed and sleep without being disturbed, and the parents could spend their evening in the light-filled house.

'With the sky, the sea and the heath, we built the houses as simply as possible, ascetically, and we were of the opinion that the heath demanded this purism,' Per Friberg says. The construction is an unpretentious framework which sets limits on nature but allows it to flow without hindrance right up to the wooden boundaries. Mountain ashes (*Sorbus aucuparia*), the climbing Italian honeysuckle (*Lonicera caprifolium*), ferns and grasses form the lower level of ground cover, over which arch the branches of the pine trees.

Per Friberg continues: 'We sit on a wooden deck in a house which is only one small thing in the middle of nature, in its simple geometry a contrast to nature's organic formal richness, but one in which its basic material, the creosoted pine wood, merges with the ground and the vegetation. It stands light and airy, insubstantial as it were with its glass front subordinated to nature.'

This airy construction has paid off for, in contrast to other houses in the area, after four decades it is still free from damp which can cause rot. And here on a beautiful summer's day you can really enjoy everything around you.

For twenty years Per Friberg was Professor of Landscape Architecture at the Universities of Lund and Alnarp and, as a leading architect and landscape architect in Sweden, designed and carried out more than seven hundred projects. Among these were power stations, with their surrounding landscapes; chapels and cemeteries, such as those at Jakobsberg and Augerum; and, on a much smaller scale, many private houses and their gardens. Despite his advanced years he is still involved with new and exciting tasks. His garden in Bjärred on Öresund, has light and dark spaces and giant yew sculptures set behind a graphic lawn display of mown and unmown grass. It is a garden for constant experimentation, with solutions that are in the first instance provisional but mature like good wine. His sense for the genuine, for the harmony of nature, landscapes, gardens and architecture produces masterpieces – like the two poetic houses set beneath the pine trees with the sea on the horizon across the heath.

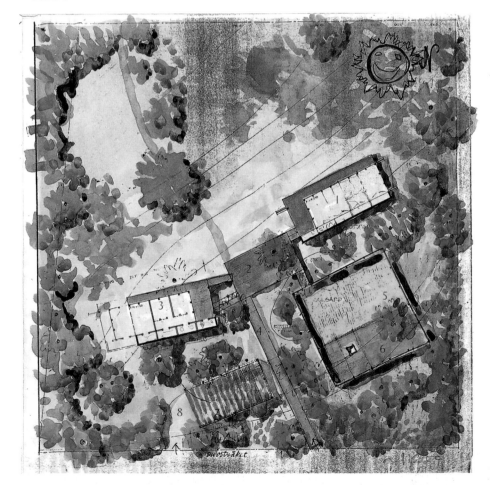

LEFT Apart from the two houses and terrace the site includes a grassy space for ball games, an area fenced in with planking for sunbathing and a space for parking. A timber path runs from the platform into the forest.

1 first house	5 fenced area
2 platform	6 barbecue
3 second house	7 sunbathing area
4 path to the forest	8 parking

RIGHT ABOVE Between the two houses there is a wide wooden platform – a sun deck with a table and benches; it leads via bridges to the slightly higher terraces in front of the two houses. A few trees were cut down to create more light since the houses are open to the east, south and west. Large windows give open views to the heath and the forest; light, white blinds provide privacy as and when required.

RIGHT BELOW From the terrace there is a gangway leading to a fenced-off courtyard area. The wooden walls are constructed of vertical boards (preserved with creosote) and are fixed to a metal framework which also supports the sliding door.

ABOVE Our tour begins in the comfortable, enclosed sitting area with light rattan chairs adjacent to the shady inner courtyard. Figs ripen above and the light and darker pinks of English and Swedish 'Morbacka' pelargoniums (named after the house of the gardener Selma Lagerlöf) are set along a window ledge that is framed by ivy.

Triangular Tapestry

A flowering island in a sea of corn and grazing land hides behind high hedges and dark fences. Only the white roses and lavender hedges in front of the bright white-washed house on the remote country road between Ystad and Trelleborg reveal our destination. Here in Äspönas, only a few miles north-east of Sweden's most southerly coast near Smygehamn, in Skåne, landscape architect Barbara Johnson and artist Botvid Kihlman have laid out their joint garden.

When Botvid bought two dilapidated semi-detached houses in 1980 on a triangular site, next to a disused railway line, it was the start of three years of hard work for him, altering and modernizing the property. Originally built for agricultural workers, the pair of small houses, separated by a dividing wall and with small rooms and tiny kitchens, was to be made into a single home with the space reallocated to suit the needs of the new owners. Rotten beams were renewed, walls pulled down and new walls built. Now generous rooms, spacious alcoves and a light veranda with rattan chairs make for an air of comfort.

Barbara received the honoured commission of designing a garden in the spirit of Emma Lundberg, Sweden's Gertrude Jekyll, and turning it into a reality which reflects the style and plants used by this pioneer. (Emma Lundberg influenced the garden culture of Sweden, especially in the 1920s and 1930s with her own garden in Lidingö, her commissioned work and her seminal books.) But here, Barbara and Botvid have each realized their own wishes and feelings.

Each of the four garden areas is a small world in itself, reserved for a few characteristic plants as favoured guests. But box, growing freely or shaped in spheres, is to be found everywhere. It mediates between the various spaces and the colours of the rich selection of perennials, the roses and the healthy vegetables and, as a common rural species, it reminds

Äspönas, Sweden

LEFT Next to the pond is an area of pinkish lilac-coloured natural stone from the Island of Öland with pockets of planting: pale blue flax (*Linum*), the crimson red of maiden pinks (*Dianthus deltoides*) and a mass of scented lavender, which likes dry conditions and a lot of sun.

RIGHT A wisteria-covered pergola with a raised area for fuchsias and other potted plants leads to the greenhouse built by Botvid in 1982. Here orange-yellow Indian mallow (*Abutilon*) blossoms and tomatoes and melons grow.

us that we are in Skåne, in the middle of the countryside. As we wander through the garden, we also come across clematis, flowering in various colours at different times of the year, on trellis, fruit trees and buildings.

The hedges, in screening and dividing up the space, give essential protection against the wind that is always sweeping across the flat countryside of the southern plain of Skåne from one direction or another. While Botvid brought a preference for evergreen trees and shrubs and other plants from his journeys in southern Provence, Barbara, who comes from Germany, is more reserved towards conifers in the countryside, with the exception of yew, she prefers deciduous trees with their changing foliage and scope for including in a balanced community of plants in which flowering perennials play a large role. Botvid previously had a different garden in this area in which conifers in shining yellow and blue colours determined the overall picture in front of white walls and pergolas. It had an atmosphere of southern Europe, which expressed his longing to be there in winter. The warm, optimistic yellow and red tones with a dash of blue and violet melancholy, can also be found in his beautiful paintings. Though inspired by nature and the garden, they are not solidly 'true to nature'. He likes to quote Edvard Munch: 'I do not paint what I see, but what I have seen.'

The garden between the studio and the guest house is a courtyard, where a large, gnarled pear tree gives shade. An ash-leaved maple (*Acer negundo*), which has whitish-green leaves that shine against the sunlight in the late afternoon and grow transparent, is the dominating feature in this setting with its atmosphere of peace. Contrasting with the inner courtyard is the largest space, which is also the most southerly, with a water-lily pond situated in the centre, a sunny sitting area, a

greenhouse and a pergola covered with wisteria; it possesses an almost Mediterranean atmosphere. This effect is strengthened by an abundance of pots and tubs with white and red fuchsias and later with the splendid blue of African lilies (*Agapanthus*). At the end of a yew hedge, which marks off the pond garden from the outer kitchen and flower garden, there is a wooden gazebo, also painted dark blue. It is a charming structure for climbing plants and contains a small bench for contemplation. The dark blue colour of the gazebo, as well as that of the fences and trellis, fits in discreetly with the colour of the flowers, seemingly detached but warmer than black or even white that blinds in sunshine.

From the southern water garden, one arrives in a different little world behind the yew hedge where tasty vegetables and lettuces are mixed with bush roses, Madonna lilies (*Lilium candidum*), lavender and silver-grey mugwort (*Artemisia*). Varieties of clematis and climbing roses are in flower on the dark blue trellis. A bench invites the visitor to stay and look. This space, full of scents and butterflies, is a happy mixture of charm and usefulness just as in genuine country cottage gardens, but with a generous touch of artistic elegance. Despite the richness of the colour, compositions are balanced and invite peaceful contemplation, here as in the other gardens, from their seats that are sometimes in sunshine, sometimes in shade.

We return to the shadow kingdom of the inner courtyard, which catches the evening light. Here, sitting on a bench surrounded by ivy, bishop's mitre (*Epimedium*) and Christmas roses (*Helleborus niger*), we can end our tour of these beautiful gardens that are all so different from one another.

OPPOSITE Three picturesque dark red cherry plum trees (*Prunus cerasifera* 'Nigra') next to the greenhouse burst into flame in the evening sun.

RIGHT Barbara Johnson and Botvid Kihlman together worked out a plan for their garden of about a quarter-acre (1000 square metres), and gradually set about turning it into reality. Four main areas are separated by trellis or hedges: a small, shady inner courtyard; a south-facing area with a pond and greenhouse; a garden for vegetables, herbs, roses and perennials; and an early summer garden for bush peonies and varieties of plantain lily (*Hosta*). Other leafy areas cater for plants for shade.

main house

1 inner courtyard with fountain and perennials for shade
2 old pear tree
3 indoor sitting area
4 studio & verandah
5 greenhouse & workshop
6 pergola
7 pond garden
8 gazebo
9 shade gardens
10 early summer garden for bush peonies (moutan)
11 vegetable garden
12 compost

Romantic Glades in Summer Land

The painter Sten Dunér's garden is in a clearing surrounded by bright birch trees, hidden deep in the forests of Småland. The Dunér family, who come from Lidingö, near Stockholm, call their place in the country 'Sommarland'. It looks at first sight like an ancient Swedish settlement in miniature, with the wooden house and huts painted a subdued rust-red and dwarfed by huge trees. This warm but unobtrusive red with its beautiful patina harmonizes with the landscape; it is called 'faluröd', and the pigment, derived from iron oxide, is named after the town of Falun. It is used a lot in Sweden and here it unites all the buildings in the garden.

Katarina and Sten's house, where they meet up with their long grown-up children and their friends, is guarded by two giant sycamores. All and sundry, family or visitors, find ample accommodation in a comfortable hut close by and in the converted barn that serves as the studio.

The garden is a sheer work of art; everything, down to the chicken house for the clucking hens, was planned to the last detail with the same care. Painted in the same rust-red, the hen-house copies in miniature the other buildings.

Besides this plot of land, which is about two-and-a-half acres (one hectare) in size, the Dunér family have leased some 7 acres (3 hectares) or so of the forest and meadows to look after the surrounding landscape and preserve its characteristics. They maintain clear views by mowing and cutting back the trees and bushes; the prospects unite the near and the distant.

Many years ago Dunér painted a view of the house seen from the front, but with small differences which baffle the viewer and which later turn out to be a key to the understanding of his magical garden. The picture consists of four parts with the two trees in the middle, in between each pair of parts, but in each a different light falls on the house and landscape. On the left, in the first section of the picture, close to the lilac hedge, a thunderstorm is brewing above the trees that are still bathed in bright light. On a white bench in front of the hedge there is a strange white ball. In the second section, in the shade on the right, we can see the black outline of a small child in the half-opened white side-door. The third part of the picture is bathed in full sunshine and once again there is the same little figure, now recognizable as a girl sitting on a swing, but this time she is close to the main door. The fourth section is also full of sunshine but is lyrical, with the softer forms of the hedges; once more the mysterious white ball is seen, hovering on the right-hand side of the picture. Using the artistic technique of 'alienation' (whereby a simple or ordinary object is transformed or 'heightened', by being placed in an unusual or unfamiliar way), the painter has brought an uncanny and even disturbing atmosphere into the picture, hinting at something threatening the idyll. It is like a symphony in four movements that shows Sten Dunér's inner state of mind, his feelings for his beloved home and garden and for his small daughter Veronika; although she is safe in her smallness under the canopy of the trees, one feels she is also in need of protection.

In the garden, as in the painting, one comes across things that 'alienate' and surprise, or simply invite one to stand and contemplate in this forest-clearing garden, with its views to adjacent meadows. Stones, especially, brought to the surface generations ago from the working of this poor soil, have now been strangely placed. Here and there a blue-painted stone indicates a place – in the grass, at the edge of the pond or on a rock – which becomes imbued with some magic quality, and so changes the perception of the visitor as well. Stones painted white serve as points of orientation in the distance and link up with nearer ones in the garden. The simple white bench in front of the lilac hedge is repeated also in the shade of the trees or shines out on a rocky slope in the dark forest.

This 'magic realism', as the artist calls it, uses simple objects to reveal 'hidden' messages, rather like the method employed by the eighteenth-century Romantic poets and painters. The German writer Novalis (1772–1801), for example, wrote that by giving a lofty meaning to the commonplace, a mysterious dignity to the normal, the value of the unknown to things we

RIGHT The main house, reached along a path bordered by red- and blackcurrant bushes, looks from a distance like a dolls' house beneath the mighty sycamore trees (*Acer pseudoplatanus*). Note, to the left, the white pedestal with a transparent, almost ethereal, glass ball on top.

Värnamo, Småland, Sweden

know, or the radiant appearance of infinity to the finite, we can endow such things with a symbolic, Romantic quality.

A more practical example of Dunér's 'land art' is across the lawn where a white net has been strung for badminton. The edges of the square playing area are marked by a strip of unmown grass, a clever solution involving a minimum of effort.

A gilded ball on the black roof of the summerhouse sparkles in the last rays of the sun and this is repeated a few yards farther on in the lawn on a white wooden post. This post stands in the middle of a bright blue, round bed of horned violets (*Viola cornuta*). From here the summerhouse with the gilded glass ball is clearly visible on a rocky rise and a few metres farther on is the delicate white wooden railing of a small bridge over a pond, looking rather as Claude Monet might have seen it, instead of here, in the middle of Sweden. Our eyes move over the small mirror-like surface of the water and the purple-red flower spikes of loosestrife (*Lythrum virgatum*) to a herb garden surrounded by hedges. It stands out clearly against the background meadow, with its small green house and hops climbing up long poles.

In choosing the plants for the garden, Dunér confined himself especially to the genuine old kinds from the area, which he collected from gardens that had long been abandoned: perennials such as campion (*Lychnis chalcedonica*), peonies, bleeding hearts and shrubs such as flowering raspberry (*Rubus odoratus*) and the spiny 'hedgehog' rose (*Rosa rugosa*). There are bushes of red-, white- and blackcurrants, gooseberry bushes, and yellow and red raspberries everywhere in the garden, often growing together with flowers. He surprises us with a combination of gooseberries, larkspur (*Consolida*) and

monkshood (*Aconitum napellus*), or horseradishes with blue irises. He does not accept the division between ornamental plants and plants for the kitchen garden and takes delight in the beauty of rhubarb leaves or uses currant bushes for hedges. Half-wild, jungle-like beds spread between the stones of this uneven terrain, separated by colour: yellow flowers on their own and blue flowers on their own. Foxgloves and lupins have unlimited freedom, whereas he severely cuts back old spiraea shrubs and even birches with his shears, shaping them into spheres and pyramids. Here, the almost untouched nature of Småland is played off against the topiary of Versailles; the gardener treads lightly between great care, boundless freedom and severe intervention:

'I do things just the way they occur to me. I like digging up perennials and planting them somewhere else in the middle of summer during the dry season; when the plant has got used to the change it is then very happy about the sudden amount of water later on. Most of this works out well. But I visit them and give them some wood ash from the stove, some fine earth from fresh molehills. Every morning I do my rounds, pull up some weeds, tie up the honeysuckle or the hops, make a new bird bath or add something to the stone wall which is already a few hundred metres long.'

In the course of time Dunér has turned his attention to the bordering forest. He has freed gnarled, moss-covered, old 'stone heads' from the vegetation that engulfed them; he has planted ferns and brought them on; he has awakened afresh the sleeping beauty of the forest. Green cushions of moss and a carpet of light grey lichen are islands on the naked stone, asking

LEFT A fixed point in this romantic island in the forest is the summer house, seen from a glade with moss-covered rocks across the lawn. Here the evening twilight can be enjoyed with a cup of tea or one can stay in close proximity to the rain pattering down outside. One can even spend a long summer night here, when in the clear moonlight nature comes into its own, untrammelled by inessentials.

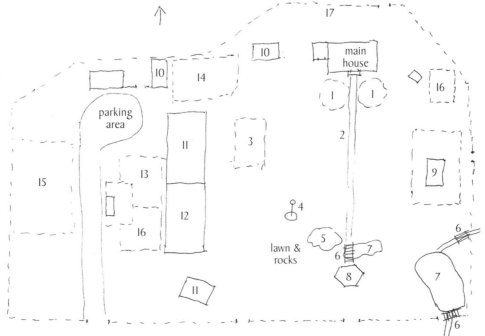

1 two giant sycamores
2 path with redcurrant bushes
3 badminton court
4 gilded glass ball on post
5 old birch tree
6 bridges
7 ponds
8 summerhouse
9 greenhouse & herb garden
10 family houses
11 guest house
12 studio
13 flower garden
14 vegetable garden
15 orchard
16 potato patches
17 boundary fence

ABOVE Lawn alternating with areas of rock. On the
left the studio, a former barn; in the lawn, the
badminton court is marked off by a rectangle of
unmown grass: land art, surrounded by freely
growing nature and shapes formed with shears.

LEFT ABOVE A greenhouse stands in the rectangle of
the herb garden. In summer hops weave up the
long poles that surround this building, their
vertical forms standing out clearly before the
landscape of the glade. In the foreground on the
edge of the pond a blue-painted stone speaks its
silence. It harmonizes with the pink colour of the
tall loosestrife (*Lythrum virgatum*), setting up a
dialogue with it.

LEFT BELOW A further small pretty garden with
precise beds of vegetables and herbs forms a
strong contrast to the adjacent meadow in August
with its reddish-golden grasses.

RIGHT A wooden bridge crosses a small brook that
runs through the property and the larger of the two
ponds. The herb garden and greenhouse are in the
background.

53

to be contemplated close up. On top of the slope one is attracted by a comb of fine, reddish, glimmering grasses.

When Sten Dunér first visited the ruined house in the woods forty years ago, nature had almost taken everything back. Only snowberries, a few old contorted apple trees and here and there some daffodils showed that human beings had once occupied this land. In the nineteenth century Johan Dröm, a professional soldier, lived here after receiving a piece of land from the state in order to grow his potatoes and carrots, and a few flowers, when he was on leave. His name speaks volumes, since 'dröm' in Swedish means 'dream'. From that time the abandoned spot in the woods was called in the local dialect 'Drömmens', and the Dunér family have kept this poetic sounding name for their 'Sommarland', which is indeed a place out of this world.

A painter, art historian and philosopher, Sten Dunér begins his book *Trådgardar* (*Gardens*) with a quotation from Thomas Aquinas: '*Habet homo rationem et manum*' ('Man possesses reason and hands'), and that certainly seems true for his garden. Following a vision, he has fashioned it with common sense, a feeling for what nature has to offer, and with hard manual work, year in, year out; so by employing both intervention and great deal of care, he has indeed brought it close to his dream.

ABOVE The boundary is formed by a rust-red batten running from post to post, a hint of a fence along the forest path, or between the woodland and meadows, as a long, light, red line, hovering between the functional and the artistic. RIGHT An idyll of moss-covered rocks and green spaces lies at the heart of the land of dreams.

Rocks, Mosses and Berries

Helsinki in August. A short journey eastwards in a small motor boat brings us to Mölandet, where Tom and Maj Simons have their summer paradise. The path leads up through a pine-wood to an inviting wooden house. The side where the front door is looks lilac-red in the sunshine with its white-framed windows, but reddish-brown in the shade. On the north side the house clings to a beautiful moss-covered rock, which can be studied more closely from the kitchen window. A short walk in a north-easterly direction leads to an attractive open mountain plateau covered with moss and grey lichen. The Simons family's property, consisting of an almost four-acre (one-and-a-half hectare) strip of mostly pine and beech wood, runs along low sea cliffs that slope down to the shore, with scree and wild vegetation. A courtyard and a half-wild garden around the house take up less than a tenth of the whole site.

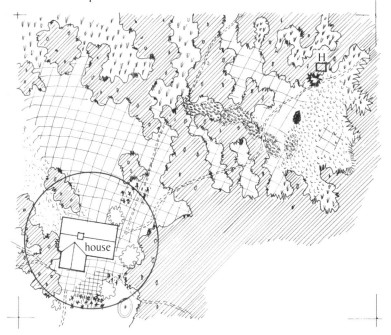

ABOVE The house is less than 50 metres (200 feet) from the seashore, and stands among pine trees, rocks and wild vegetation. The circle describes the garden with its plants and mosses that are cultivated around the house.

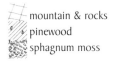 mountain & rocks
pinewood
sphagnum moss

 *Polytrichum*
scrub & bilberries
H hut (privy)

Tom Simons, a landscape architect with a professorial post in the Department of Architecture at the Helsinki University of Technology, has served as Visiting Professor at the Royal Danish Academy of Fine Arts and at the Graduate School of Design at Harvard University. He is currently engaged on research into urban parks in Finland. Tom told me the history of the house, which starts in the 1930s. For two generations it belonged to another family until Tom's father bought the property in 1985. He began to modernize the house, putting in electricity and drilling a well, but died soon after he had started the work. After his death, the family completed the modernization. Among other things, they added two windows to the north side of the house, one in the big room and one in the kitchen.

A few years ago Maj and Tom bought out the shares of his mother, brothers and sisters, who acquired the neighbouring house. Maj and Tom call their house and the land, which previously had no name, simply 'Mølandet' after the island; it means 'virgin land'. Maj, who works as an editor for radio, says that the older generation of the previous owners used to have a garden of many flowers, with paths of natural stone and a kitchen garden with a potato field; it was they who made the small terraces, which are now covered with beautiful moss. But the younger generation did not look after the garden and vegetation, especially raspberry bushes, had spread everywhere by the time Tom's father bought the property. Among the inventory of old plants that Maj listed were ancient, but luxuriantly flowering, lilac bushes; elephant's ears (*Bergenia*); masses of foxgloves; dark red, strongly scented bush roses; pale blue monkshood (*Aconitum napellus*); and wild, orange hawkweed (*Pilosella aurantiaca*) with its shining, orange-yellow flowers that form thick natural mats.

Maj and Tom are great lovers of nature, the pines, the stones, the various types of moss, the countless kinds of grass and small wild pansies, speedwell (*Veronica*) and last but not

RIGHT A picturesque pine shaped by the wind, the stony rockface with a green cushion of bear moss (*Polytrichum commune*). Robust elephant's ears (*Bergenia cordifolia*) spread out in the sun on a bank by the Simons family's house.

Island of Mölandet, near Helsinki

ABOVE Sphagnum moss, which can be reddish in colour.

BELOW Lichen-covered granite rock.

BELOW The red pearls of cranberries.

least *Epilobium*, the willow herb, which if it were not wild, would count as one of the most beautiful bedding perennials.

Tom now tells the story of his moss garden. 'When we had settled in here in the summer, we started to see the rich treasure of mosses around us. During the first summer we read Tove Jansson's *Summerbook* with its descriptions of the same kind of natural surroundings on the islands of the Skärgården as here on Mölandet. The book provided us with rules of conduct, which we tried in a roundabout way to get our guests to accept.' On mosses, Tove Jansson, Finland's most successful woman writer (whose books have been translated into twelve languages and who is especially famous for her 'Moomin' books), writes: 'Only farmers and summer visitors walk on the moss. They do not know and it cannot be said often enough that moss is the most sensitive plant that there is. You step on it once and the moss recovers in the rain, but the second time it does not. The third time you walk over the moss it is dead.'

In their second and third summers, Tom Simons started deliberately to clean and weed the mosses. He chose two places, the rocky eminence in front of the kitchen window and a beautifully open mountain plateau to the north-east. This, with a diameter of some 20 metres (70 feet), is for the most part covered with lichen, the moss *Polytrichum commune*, heather and bilberries. Another, lighter moss that prefers damp conditions flows down over the rock from a higher mountain ridge onto a lower plateau, where the light green mat peters out in a curve and forms round green islands on the rocks which are covered with light grey lichen. The moss looks like a stream or glacier that is flowing into a small lake with islands, a miniature landscape. The botanical name of this bog moss, which follows the water channels, is *Sphagnum capillifolium* (syn. *S. nemorcum*); called in Swedish *tallvitmossa* ('pine white moss'), it thrives here in the light shadow of the pines. (Swedish is the mother tongue of the Simons family as is the case with a small part of Finland's population, especially on the coast.) In some places on the moss reddish tones can be seen. This difference in colour may have formed as a result of varying exposure to the sun and different degrees of dampness; however, it probably comes from other varieties of sphagnum moss that are naturally red such as the rust-red *Sphagnum fuscum* or the purplish-red *S. warnstorfianum*. But the final word would have to be

RIGHT The most beautiful scene in Tom Simons' moss garden is under the pine trees: *Sphagnum capillifolium*, a moss that likes damp conditions, flows out between rocks covered with grey lichen down to a lower plateau of the cliff following the line of the rain water.

THE CARE AND PLANTING OF MOSSES

A moss garden is a new small world waiting to be discovered. It can be shaped with one's own ideas without having to resort to Japanese garden culture, but the centuries-old practical experience and the gardening skill of Japanese moss experts with the same moss species that grow in our own climes is extremely valuable.

Since moss in pots cannot be purchased at garden centres in our part of the world, we are dependent on moss in the wild, but of course not from nature reserves. In any case, to gather moss one should always have the permission of the owner of the land and limit oneself to small pieces from the most common varieties to keep the damage to the area of moss to a minimum. It will regenerate after a year or two. The best time to transplant moss is early spring or late autumn, when evaporation is at its lowest.

Moss generally does not like too much direct sunlight but requires partial shade, for example under a pergola or tree or in the shadow of a wall. Coniferous trees give shade the whole year round, deciduous trees less so in the months when they have lost their leaves. The light requirements vary, however, with different species. Most mosses like acid soil with a pH of between 6 and 6.5 that is constantly damp but not wet, with the exception of varieties of sphagnum moss that like to have 'wet feet'. One can generally say for mosses that the more acceptable the ground and the dampness, the better they will put up with a lighter position.

Suitable varieties for gardens are especially those that grow in acid soil and so have less competition from weeds, for example varieties of polytrichum, which are native to Scandinavia. In Swedish they are called 'bjornmossar'; in Norwegian 'björnemose' ('bear mosses'); and in German 'Haarmützenmoos' ('hair cap moss'). Botanically speaking sphagnum and polytrichum belong to the order of the Bryales in contrast to the Andreaeales, or slit mosses, which do not have proper roots and leaves. They are used in the moss gardens in Japan especially because of their beautifully sculptured forms. The most common 'bear moss' *Polytrichum commune* requires less shade, grows tall and loses its shape; it can be trimmed just like the other polytrichum varieties; *P. juniperinum* will even put up with dry, sandy soil.

The wind-blown moss (*Dicranum scoparium*) is widespread in the raw leaf mould of the woodland floor and on stony mountainous terrain with its shoots, 3-10 centimetres (1-4 inches) in length, joined to form beautiful pale green carpets. In the shade of deciduous trees and best of all in peat-based beds the pin-cushion moss (*Leucobryum glaucum*) produces soft, half-domed, bluish-white to green cushions. This moss with its clearly formed dense head also grows well in a terracotta pot. Sphagnum

moss for a bed of wet peat changes at times from green to reddish shades: *S. fuscum* is rust-red and *S. warnstorfianum* is purplish-red. In dry conditions sphagnum takes on a whitish colour, which is caused by the cells absorbing a lot of air. For this reason it is also called white moss.

When transferring mosses from the wild to the garden, attention should be given to the following: remove small pieces from the moss cover with their roots intact and, if possible for optimum conditions, with a few centimetres of earth from around their natural position. This enormously facilitates their taking in their new surroundings. Since mosses do not have a pronounced root system, they can easily be removed. Then rake smooth the earth in the bed intended for the mosses. A layer of loam or peaty soil, some 15 centimetres (6 inches) deep, is sufficient. Pure peat is also ideal, but sandy soils are less suitable, because they dry out more quickly. Keep the bed free of weeds; on no account should fertilizer be used. Before planting, water the bed well and moisten well the top and underside of the moss. Press the moss on to the earth so that it makes good contact with it. The moss can be cut into smaller pieces so that a larger surface area can then be covered with small pieces. These must be well-watered, because smaller pieces dry out more easily. The bare earth has to be covered with peat that has not been fertilized so that the moss has contact with the earth on all sides. During the first weeks the moss must be watered several times a day so that it can anchor itself and take.

When transplanting moss on to a stone in the shade, a useful method is to use ordinary wallpaper paste to stick the moss on to the stone; then, during the following weeks, spray it daily with water.

Some gardens in Japan contain ancient polytrichum moss that has grown proper stems and is regularly pruned. Cultivated moss can grow so strongly that the stems do not get enough air and may rot, and it is therefore important that moss plants, particularly when young, should regularly be loosened up and 'combed' with a coarse rake; fallen leaves and weeds should also be removed so that salutary air can get at them.

Natural areas of moss are an important gift that one should perhaps appreciate more. Many mosses thrive in towns, as the famous moss gardens in the metropolis of Kyoto with its millions of inhabitants prove. Varieties of polytrichum, which, it seems, are also resistant to strong air pollution, are favourites in Japan and, common as they are in northern Europe, their qualities make them well suited to our gardens, especially in cities. In Japan mosses can be bought at the nursery, so why should we too not make more use of them in our garden designs and indeed make them more commercially available as exciting plants to grow?

pronounced by a moss expert who could identify the different species on the spot with a magnifying glass. The most beautiful red, however, is provided by the cranberries, which have established themselves with a small bush in the middle of the sphagnum moss and bed their shining sun-drenched pearls on the green cushion. The umbrellas of a few catchfly toadstools look as if they were painted on the silver-grey carpet of lichen, just like the bluish-grey lichen on the pale lilac rock.

To look after his moss garden, this true gift of nature, which is some 300 square yards (250 square metres) in size, Tom Simons collects up all the pine cones and dry twigs and brushes away the pine needles from the green carpet with a small sweeping brush, especially when it is dry. He plucks out blades of grass, removing by hand tufts of grass, the common polypody fern (*Polypodium vulgare*), stonecrop (*Sedum*) and other plants that might disturb the moss. Tom leaves the small wild pansy, heartsease (*Viola tricolor*), that some years is in abundance, to flower in the cushion of moss. 'The fantastic thing about mosses,' says Tom, 'is that they give us so much for relatively little work. A new world of wonderful shapes opens up, finely balanced colour combinations and fascinating fine borders between the naked rock and the moss cover. It is not necessary

to make direct connections between such miniature landscapes and the well-known Japanese gardens. I see them rather as a rich part of our nature. My moss garden rests on creating awareness and understanding of nature with the help of my hands. But I do not see it as a crime to add new elements to such a landscape. Cleaning and bringing order with a light touch is already something alien to nature, that is already the start of human interference. Why not continue along these lines, if we have understanding for the fantastic small world of mosses? As a small, final memento on our proud but vulnerable 'glacier' I have added a new artificial island with a species of stonecrop that has been growing on Mölandet for a long time and two small yew bushes on the outer edge where the sphagnum moss has already formed islands.'

Shortly after my visit to the Island of Mölandet a moss expert from Taiwan approached Tom Simons with a request to be allowed to see and study this rich collection of moss species on the spot. But the weather changed dramatically so that the crossing in the small motorboat had to be cancelled. When one considers that large parts of Scandinavia, especially Finland, Sweden and Norway, are covered with mosses, there is evidently scope for plenty of botanical discoveries in this field.

ABOVE Tubs, hanging baskets and planting have been carefully chosen to enliven the yellow façade of the new-looking wooden house, approached through the garden along a gently winding, grey-cobbled path.

BELOW In the immediate vicinity of the house two trees, a mature lime and a younger horse chestnut, stand out against the backdrop of an evergreen hedge.

Nature Garden in Fields & Woods

A slightly curved path crosses the lawn, past a chestnut tree and a taller lime tree, up to a yellow friendly-looking wooden house. In the middle its red-tiled roof drops down to protect a veranda full of flowers. Here and by the path to the entrance, we are immediately greeted by a colourful array, dominated by a large clump of yellow sundrops (*Oenothera fruticosa* subsp. *glauca*).

This house in Degernes, to the south of Oslo, is the home of the landscape architect Nils Skaarer and his wife Sigrid, and their two grown-up sons Anders Martin and John Fredrik. The garden, a quarter-acre (1150 square metres) in size, together with a large and ancient rust-red barn, forms part of the family's farm of some 40-odd acres (17 hectares). It is situated in an interesting and varied landscape with dark woods to the west, and a few silver birches to the east, which brighten up the edge of the woodland. Between the woods and the garden there is an open-edged, bright cornfield, a peaceful background against which the structures of the garden stand out attractively. A few rocky outcrops in the landscape of ploughed fields combine picturesquely with trees. Nils Skaarer took this scenery into consideration in planning the garden, and by leaving part of the boundary open to the landscape he incorporated it into his garden picture.

The outer framework of the garden therefore consists of a loosely planted mixture of shrubs with trees here and there. Their resistance to cold is tested here in the interior of Østfold, some 30 kilometres (18 miles) from the coast and 115 metres (380 feet) above sea level, with frequent night frosts in spring and autumn. This area registers a hardiness rating of Z5 in Norway. These periods of low temperatures, with which you have to reckon here, limit the choice of varieties, which start to produce shoots and then suffer a shock and damage on a cold night. That is the case with a number of shrubs such as the snowball tree (*Viburnum opulus* 'Roseum') and perennials such

Degernes, Rakkestad, Norway

ABOVE Behind tall, slender racemes of bright yellow *Ligularia stenocephala* is the subdued dark purple-red of a smallish copper beech that still looks like a dense bush and forms a surprisingly effective background for the yellows. The refreshing white of mullein (*Verbascum*) is close by; and a little further away a mock orange (*Philadelphus pubescens*), which grows up to 16 feet (5 metres) tall and here in Norway is hardier than the common *P. coronarius*, rounds off this flower bed by the veranda. It can easily be seen from the house and from a distance, and makes an effective backdrop for the medium-sized perennials.

LEFT In July, the luxuriant yellow of a large clump of sundrops (*Oenothera tetragona* subsp. *glauca*), an extremely rewarding long-flowering perennial, dominates in the front of the bed and beneath it a white carpet of the flowers of stonecrop (*Sedum album*) and a crimson patch of maiden pinks (*Dianthus deltoides*), which was grown from seed.

63

as astilbe and lilies. And it can still happen in late May, even in June, when frost is no longer expected. Early spring flowers, especially bulbs, rarely suffer in this way. Even the late autumn is not frost free in some years. Asters and especially gentians (*Gentiana sino-ornata*) can tolerate some cold, but black snake-root (*Cimicifuga racemosa*) cannot tolerate any cold at all and is sometimes killed off before it can flower. Nils set great store by autumnal tints in his choice of bushes, such as the shadbush (*Amelanchier canadensis*), varieties of berberis, spindle tree (*Euonymus europaeus*), *Spiraea betulifolia* in the compact variety 'Umeå' with its red foliage in the autumn (good for the rockery, for example) and finally red-barked dogwood (*Cornus alba* 'Sibirica'), that captivates us in the winter with its intense red shoots. There is the scent of many bushes throughout the year, such as that of the hardy mock orange (*Philadelphus*), the common lilac (*Syringa vulgaris*), the common honeysuckle (*Lonicera periclymenum*), the early-flowering mezereon (*Daphne mezereum*) and the later *Viburnum carlesii*, which both have a heady sweet fragrance.

ABOVE The comfortable veranda with its white rattan furniture has a decorative floral display that greets the visitor from afar, an enticing invitation to come and see the fresh-looking plants from close up. Pansies in tubs and baskets show a happy, natural mixture of plants that are planted at the beginning of April before they show any colour. In the hanging flower-pots and boxes on the posts, summer annuals are in flower, pink *Diascia barberae* and blue *Scaevola saligna*, and also pansies have been used again. Bridging the gap between the veranda and a single window is a dwarf willow (*Salix purpurea* 'Nana'). All these details enliven the yellow façade.

BELOW LEFT An outline map of the whole property in its rural setting of fields and woods. The house and large barn next to the gravel parking area are approached along a curving driveway.
BELOW An enlarged plan of the garden inset left, showing the main planting areas – trees and shrubs, and the perennial and five-seasons beds.

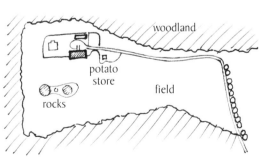

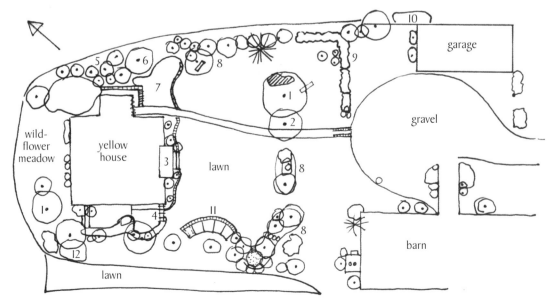

1 horse chestnut
2 lime tree
3 veranda
4 pergola with hop
5 currants & gooseberries
6 beech

7 perennial border
8 shrubs and small trees
9 evergreen hedge
10 compost
11 five-seasons border
12 apple trees

Yet this garden that harmonizes with the fields and the woods was also planned according to ecological considerations. Among the bushes with delicate fruits for birds (which are after all a part of the atmosphere of paradise) are the common snowberry (*Symphoricarpos*), the juneberry (*Amelanchier spicata*) with its blue-black berries, the reddish-purple-leaved barberry (*Berberis ottawensis* 'Superba') with an abundance of red berries, the hawthorn (*Crataegus intricata*) with brownish-red berries and the Oregon grape (*Mahonia aquifolium*) with its decorative blue-black berries, and not forgetting a red-leaved cultivar of ornamental crab apple (*Malus baccata*) with red stems and a profusion of bright red fruit. Nils has also thought of insects such as bees and butterflies which have a predilection for plants with nectar, pollen and edible leaves: bushes such as honeysuckle (*Lonicera caerulea*) and twinberry (*L. involucrata*) are small 'taverns' and no butterfly passes by the tall perennial Joe Pye weed (*Eupatorium purpureum*) with its wine-red corymb-like panicles of flowerheads. (The climate here is unfortunately too harsh for *Buddleja davidii*, the butterfly bush.) But besides nectar these charming little gliders, which enchant a summer's day, also have to ensure sufficient food for their caterpillars. The red admiral is happy with common nettles, the peacock butterfly is interested in hops as well as nettles, the Camberwell beauty prefers willows and birches for its progeny and the caterpillars of the brimstone butterfly love the foliage of alder buckthorn (*Rhamnus frangula*) and common buckthorn (*R. cathartica*).

Nils, who is conversant with biological questions, reports an interesting piece of research whereby many more kinds of insects were counted on native trees than on foreign trees. At the top of the list is the common oak (*Quercus robur*) with 300 different types of insect, followed by the willow with 260, the birch with 230, the pine with ninety and the lime tree with thirty. On foreign trees introduced into Norway there were only one to five types of insect! Whoever wants to create ecological balance in his or her garden cannot do without at least a few native trees. Trees with insects are also feeding stations for our feathered guests, who then appear five or sixfold in the garden at meal times. Nature is simply full of interconnections.

Walking through this biologically controlled garden, which as we have seen is open to the landscape, we come across a curved flower bed containing five squares, each of them one-and-a-half square metres in size, where an ornamental tub with the violet flowers of the blue potato bush (*Solanum rantonnettii*) is filling in during a gap in the flowering cycle.

ABOVE Nils Skaarer deliberately left the garden open to its surroundings to provide vistas such as this still scene of wheatfields against the vertical shapes of the pine trees. The small hut is used as a potato store.

Each of these squares is a flowering picture that changes in the course of the year. The first picture begins with crocuses, squills (*Scilla*) and trinity flowers (*Trillium*) and is called *Aprilslippet*, literally 'the April letting-out', a rural term, which refers to the wild behaviour of the cows when they are let out to graze for the first time after the winter. The last picture is a late-summer and autumnal scene with the white of phlox and black snake-root (*Cimicifuga racemosa*), orange phlox and yellow tickseed (*Coreopsis verticillata*) and blue alpine asters (*Aster alpinus*). In between, there is a square with the scent of grape hyacinths (*Muscari*) and large hyacinths, a further spring picture with Dutch tulips and a 'June 12th' bed with a bush peony, white bachelor's buttons (*Ranunculus aconitifolius* 'Flore Pleno'), and Spanish bluebells (*Hyacinthoides hispanica*), framed by pink sea thrift (*Armeria maritima*).

After this curved little garden with its five seasons we pass a pergola covered in hops, where the caterpillars of the peacock butterfly can feel at home. Then, beyond a wooden terrace, we reach the northern end of the garden behind the house where we come to a small summer flower meadow full of butterflies and the humming of bees.

ABOVE The driveway sweeps round to the entrance canopy of a long, low two-storey building that contrasts with the vertical lines of the pine trees. The trees give way to rhododendrons and lawn, with climbing shrubs along the façade.

BELOW On the plan the forest edge of the garden appears as a rampart-like structure in an irregular, broken line like a cogwheel. On the ground it is apparent as the less obvious raised edge of the lawn, where shrubs hold back the pines.

1 entrance canopy
2 rhododendron
3 *Parthenocissus inserta*
4 covered walkway & sitting area
5 pergola
6 sauna
7 swimming pool
8 white marguerites
9 *Salix alba* var. *sericea* (two remain)
10 *Berberis thunbergii* f. *atropurpurea*
11 veranda
12 stone wall with wooden benches
13 former orchard

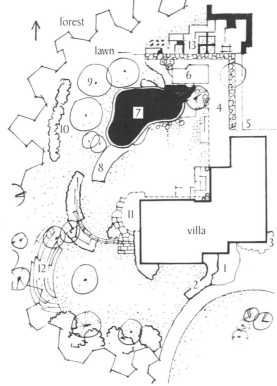

Alvar Aalto's Villa Mairea

As we drive along the road that crosses the estate's surrounding farmland we glimpse a white shape, higher up among the pine trees. The climb takes us through a scattering of rhododendron bushes until at last we can see the complex configuration of shapes and planes that make up the Villa Mairea.

We cannot, in talking about this garden, afford to ignore the villa because the two were planned together by Alvar Aalto (1898–1976), one of the great creative geniuses of our time. This work, which dates from the thirties (1938–39) is one of the highest expressions of Aalto's artistic imagination, thanks in no small measure to the good fortune that brought him two refined and wealthy clients, Harry and Maire Gullichsen. The estate at Noormarkku was to become the main residence of the Gullichsen family, visited in its time by a multitude of guests from the worlds of business, finance and the arts; today it houses the offices of the Mairea Foundation.

The villa consists of a series of regular shapes and volumes in between that are offset as a series of compact units with gentle platform roofs. This arrangement is extended by means of a covered walkway to the sauna. Within the structures, an area of lawn is enclosed by gently rising ground, which on the far side descends towards the pine-wood. Counter-balancing this higher ground, which offers protection from the north wind, is the hollow of a swimming pool, its curved shape set neatly into the lawn within a simple border of white stones. It is fed by running water. In front, a patch of white marguerites (*Leucanthemum vulgare*) provides an ideal continuation of the pool's curved shape and partly shields it from view; these were the favourite flowers of Maire Gullichsen, the muse who inspired the garden. East of the covered walkway a cantilevered logwood pergola directs our attention, with its diagonally set roof timbers, towards the forest and the morning light.

The basement level of the building is set into the hillside; the building itself stretches into the wooded countryside. The

Noormarkku, Finland

ABOVE The site occupies the crest of the hill and is surrounded by a pine-forest, which covers the whole slope as far as the bottom of the hill, where the farm belonging to the family lies. Here, the swimming pool garden nestles into the lawn with the grass-roofed sauna behind; to the right is the covered walkway between the house and sauna, also used as a sitting area. On the left of the pool is a bed of white marguerites, flowers that were loved by Maire Gullichsen, the muse who inspired the villa and garden's creation, who with her husband Harry commissioned Aalto Alvar.

ABOVE Two *Salix alba* var. *sericea* shimmer above the clear blue pool. To the left, the garden opens out to the north-west where a closely cut lawn bordered with a hedge of *Berberis thunbergii* f. *atropurpurea* (BELOW) melds with the forest. A pair of granite columns, the lighter one half-hidden in foliage, are 'King & Queen', by Norwegian sculptor Bård Broivik.

most striking feature is that its large windows at the entrance allow the entire structure of the villa to be assimilated at a glance. Light permeates the interior space, from where we can view the sparsely laid out central open area next to the pool. It is only here that there is full sun, because outside the villa the garden is characterized by patches of shade, as light must first penetrate the foliage of the pine trees surrounding the garden.

Openings and entrances incorporated into the villa's design allow for a number of different vistas across the surrounding area, emphasizing the close relationship between house and garden. Bringing it even closer, climbing plants cling to and even envelop several parts of the villa. A *Parthenocissus inserta* at the entrance porch softens the severity of its structure, while an exuberant *Actinidia kolomikta* reaches up to the wooden balcony on the first floor. It is not possible to make a clear distinction between where one part of the building starts and the plant finishes. Right under this balcony, in a corner composed of two glass walls, is the veranda, a living room with wicker chairs and a floor of stone slabs like those that continue outside. The lines of the window casings frame, section by section, tiny views of the garden, partly obscured by the large leaves of *Philodendron cordatum*.

On the little hill behind the swimming pool the silver leaves of two specimens of *Salix alba* var. *sericea* stand out against the wood, revealing the hand of the designer. They also contrast boldly with the dark wooden timbers used for the construction of the sauna (added in the early 1960s) which, with its cover of flat grass extending over the whole L-shape of the platform roof, resembles nothing so much as a primitive forest hut.

Behind the sauna is a solid stone wall, little more than a metre (3 feet) high, partially covered with moss. Recreating the traditional wall enclosure of the Finnish countryside, it separates the central part of the garden from the wood. On the opposite side the lawn assumes a more rounded form, marked off by another stone wall which emphasizes a change in level. This wall is less evident than the first as it is flanked on both sides by shrubs including a *Hydrangea anomala* subsp. *petiolaris*, which is covered with white flowers in July. A little

RIGHT A *Hydrangea anomala* subsp. *petiolaris* covers the low, curving wall next to the veranda, which is hidden from view by the mass of *Actinidia kolomikta* that climbs to the first-floor balcony. The curved shape of the wall, like that of the swimming pool, show Aalto's interest in organic forms, which contrast with the pure geometry of the house. Beyond the lawn, round stone boulders, partly covered with moss and scattered in grassy undergrowth thick with bilberry, underline the wildness of the forest area.

farther away, but before the denseness of the forest, is a long, curving hedge of *Berberis thunbergii* f. *atropurpurea*, which serves as a backdrop to the pool and helps to anchor the nearby willows.

The colour composition in the garden ranges from various shades of green to the silvery-grey of the willows, from the deep red of the berberis and the mauve of the clematis climbing the white pillars of the walkway, to the whites and yellows of the seasonal flowers, It reflects the express wishes of the lady of the house, still respected today by those charged with responsibility for the garden. Maire Gullichsen's fondness for white flowers

met with Aalto's complete approval. Embellishing the garden with flowers of the purest of colours illuminated the atmosphere, and underlined the importance of light, which was a recurring theme of the architect's vision.

The bond here between architectural structure and the spirit of the garden and its setting may best be described as intimate. No detail is left to improvization; the use of spaces is deeply thought out so that a harmony is maintained between the solid shapes and empty volumes, the materials of the villa and the garden constructions, the layout and also the plants used on the walls and in the garden.

OPPOSITE PAGE The sauna and covered area viewed from 'outside' the garden. The traditional Finnish rustic wall with its irregular-sized boulders recreates the type of enclosure found in the countryside round about. Hops (*Humulus lupulus*) covering vertical structures add to the rusticity of the scene.

RIGHT An interior with its stone-slab floor and comfortable wicker chairs, like those used outside. The windows are made up of a series of small vertical panes of glass.

ABOVE Among the tables and chairs under the white-pillared covered area are several examples of white furnishings, including the tables in the shape of a marguerite. Designed by Aalto's wife Aino in Maire's honour, they are still produced by Artek, the furnishing enterprise founded in 1935 by Maire with the architect and his wife. Beyond the lawn *Philodendron cordatum* climbs the veranda walls.

ABOVE The south side and main entrance of Kaare Frölich's house on the top of a hill.

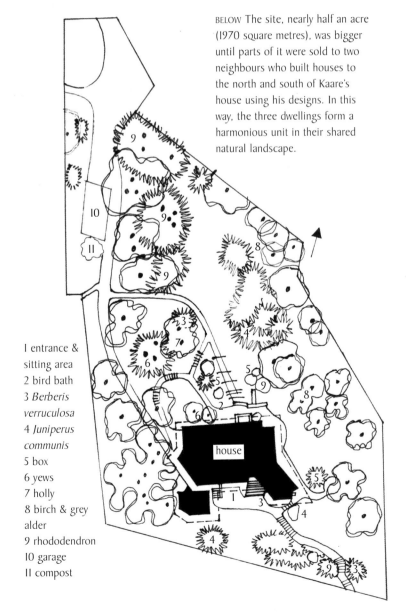

BELOW The site, nearly half an acre (1970 square metres), was bigger until parts of it were sold to two neighbours who built houses to the north and south of Kaare's house using his designs. In this way, the three dwellings form a harmonious unit in their shared natural landscape.

1 entrance & sitting area
2 bird bath
3 *Berberis verruculosa*
4 *Juniperus communis*
5 box
6 yews
7 holly
8 birch & grey alder
9 rhododendron
10 garage
11 compost

Green Hillside with Stone Paths

Bergen, July. The rain beats against the windscreen as I drive in a southerly direction to pay my first visit to Troldhaugen, once the home of Edvard Grieg (see page 116). But I have a second appointment that day, which is to meet the architect Kaare Frölich in nearby Nesttun and drive with him to his house tucked away on a hillside. Kaare speaks a clear Norwegian that I can understand, and I get along with Swedish. So we start to get acquainted before we reach the house.

The property is at the end of a small road and from a black car-port a grey gravel path leads steeply up to the dark house. On the way we pass a small wood with a few birches and grey alders (*Alnus incana*), with grey undersides to their leaves. Native trees, they are impervious to hard winters and flourish here on the damp ground. The dark brown creosoted wooden house is a structure rich in different angles and formations. On the south, main entrance side, are two wings that extend left and right towards the sun. Fortunately, the sun does put in an appearance next morning and warmth collects in this semi-courtyard, sheltered from the wind, insofar as the dark wood walls absorb the heat.

We go inside and I meet Kaare's wife Torborg, who, as a landscape architect, has long imprinted her naturalistic style on many gardens in the Bergen area. (An archive record of her work is held at the Agricultural University of Norway.) Kaare was a successful architect within the Cubus group of architects in Bergen. Among his projects in the 1960s was the design of the highly acclaimed Landåshallen, which provides two schools with large areas for physical training and swimming, and also two big estates of houses, originally intended for sailors' families. A selection of the work of this creative husband and wife duo, who are both in their eighties, was published in the 1999 Yearbook of the Norwegian Architecture Museum in Oslo. Whilst Kaare is still active and does all the shopping, Torborg has mobility

Nesttun, Bergen, Norway

ABOVE An end-on view of the dark timber house from the garage below.

RIGHT The north-facing glass living-room wall gives a fascinating panoramic view of the garden – especially the natural bird baths close to the window. Now that Torborg's movements are restricted, her enjoyment of this view is a source of strength and certainly also a reason for her cheerfulness.

ABOVE Red astilbe and pinkish-purple foxgloves, scattered with a light hand, enliven the predominantly green and restful landscape, which is dotted with sculptured rock formations and rock-edged grass paths.

73

problems but with the help of a small aid called a rollator she can walk short distances, such as to the door that leads into the north-westerly garden. They invite me to stay and so I spend four days in this comfortable house with its aromas of wood; now and again I am transformed into a cook to take my turn at the stove. We have long conversations in front of the fire in the central brick fireplace in the big, high-ceilinged living room. The all-purpose room provides enough space for working and an old grand piano for music; there is also the kitchen alcove and a dining table close by. There is a separate small room for visitors. The south wing accommodates the bathroom, a bedroom and a study added in 1981. The Frölichs have been living in this house since 1960. When Kaare originally designed it, it consisted of 1110 square feet (103.2 square metres); the study added another 180 square feet (16.8 square metres). By keeping the outside walls along the living room low, it was possible to construct a window facing north that goes from ground level to the roof using insulation glass. Central heating radiators, which would have disturbed the effect, could be eliminated, because heat radiates from the ceiling. In the cold season there is additional heat from an iron stove and the fire.

The garden that Torborg designed in 1960 to the north and south of the dark wooden house was originally full of fruit trees and had belonged to a nearby farm. The terrain consists primarily of slate, which crumbles easily and splits giving access to the soil. In the small valley to the south the earth is largely clay, whereas in the damp hollow to the north there are grey alders, sometimes growing as big bushes, bird cherries (*Prunus padus*), birches, bilberries, heather, ferns and juniper. Torborg complemented the wild vegetation here and there with rhododendrons and azaleas, and perennials between the rocks to mask the wounds caused by unavoidable blasting when the house was built. She especially planted good ground cover: yellow archangel (*Lamium galeobdolon*), with its silver markings, and masses of bergenias.

When the sky clears up I spend a few days moving restlessly like Per Gynt, between the Frölich's house and garden on its slope and Edvard Grieg's Troldhaugen. Then I take my farewells of Kaare and Torborg, worrying a little about them, but also excited by the thought of a new garden adventure that awaits me in a few hours, towards evening in the park at Rosendal, in the midst of a grandiose mountain landscape.

LEFT Looking rather endearing, like elephants' ears flapping against the bare rock, massed bergenia leaves appear to listen out for the vibrant birdsong.

ABOVE At one time the garden was an orchard, but now spindly birches and massed ground cover such as the silver carpet of lamium fill the spaces between the trees.

BELOW Ancient smoothed rock half-covered with creeping Jenny (*Lysimachia nummularia*) and a scattering of wild strawberries.

75

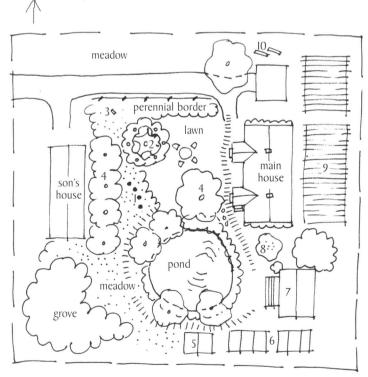

1 geese
2 grove with ancient grave
3 carved animal
4 birches
5 glasshouse

6 coldframes
7 poultry house
8 lilacs
9 vegetable garden
10 red sails

Fables, Yellow & Gold

Six wild white geese move their wings in the light breeze but continue to stay in the same place, for they are made of wood and each is attached to a light dove-blue stick. The half-dozen sticks are placed in such a way that the flock seems to be flying over a grove of the perennial giant wild parsnip (*Heracleum* sp.) among tall grasses, past a birch tree in front of a small, ochre-yellow house. The house, with its warm Norwegian Stavern-yellow exterior (the colour is named after a small town on the west coast) has a beautiful weathered tiled roof and, to left and right, two porches, each below a classic, white triangular gable. These symmetrical entrances are flanked by pots of red begonias and yellow marigolds (*Tagetes*), and in a small bed of perennials close to the first door on the left there stand the yellow flower heads of *Ligularia* 'The Rocket'. The colour yellow is repeated in several larger groups of loosestrife (*Lysimachia punctata*) which, together with the orange-yellow flowers of golden groundsel (*Ligularia dentata*), a shorter annual type of marigold and the shining orange of the tiger lily (*Lilium lancifolium*), form a bright flower bed on the edge of a largish, circular pond.

The house and garden with the warm, joyful colours belong to the Gabrielsen family. Egil and Solveig Gabrielsen had bought the property in the country in Søndre Finstad, south of Oslo, in 1972. Solveig had taught home economics and nutrition science in a school in Stabbek near Oslo. Egil, a landscape architect by profession, was until he retired Professor at the Agricultural University of Norway in nearby Ås.

Most of the house dates from 1750, although in 1918 a

Søndre Finstad, Norway

LEFT ABOVE The low entrance porches sit snugly next to the yellow spires of *Ligularia* 'The Rocket', campanulas and marigolds in a pot. The soft grass paths add to the timelessness of the scene.

LEFT BELOW The site, part of a former farm, covers an area of about one-and-a-quarter acres (some 5000 square metres).

ABOVE Egil Gabrielsen's flock of six wooden geese with their pointed, windmill-sail wings that spin in the breeze. From across the lawn their whiteness shines out but their light dove-blue posts dissolve among the greenery, so that they appear to be flying over a grove of wild parsnip.

RIGHT By the pond, hybrid cultivars of the tiger lily (*Lilium lancifolium*) shine out against yellow *Lysimachia punctata*.

FOLLOWING PAGES Morning atmosphere over the glade in front of the ochre house (LEFT). Ash trees and birches, beds with shrubs, perennials and brightly coloured summer flowers surround the well-kempt lawn which ends in a wild meadow. It is a garden interwoven with nature and the history of the farm that was here before.

The yellow and orange tones of loosestrife (*Lysimachia punctata*), various kinds of *Ligularia* and marigolds are dominant by the pond in July (RIGHT). The house of Egil's son Hein and his family is visible in the background. Every day is a holiday in this spacious, shared garden.

second loggia-style porch was added on the right. There are yellow-flowering perennials and shrubs that turn gold in autumn, warm colours that are echoed in the ochre-yellow of the former farm house. The lawn is the meeting place for the three generations of the Gabrielsen family who share the site. Solveig and Egil occupy the larger house, pictured on page 78, and across the lawn, part-hidden behind a line of birch trees, their son Hein and family have made a comfortable home for themselves in the smaller house that was once a farm labourer's cottage.

On my visit Egil takes his grandson Søndre by the hand for their customary walk together around the garden; I take a photograph of the four-year-old astride a wooden giraffe which, half-hidden behind trees, stands with its long neck and small head on a meadow close to Egil's windmill-winged geese on their dove-blue posts. Together we also discover a horse, a dog and a cat, which Søndre's clever grandfather had made in a similar way from various pieces of wood. (A second series of Egil's wooden animals stands as fixed sculptures along a public path in the nearby town of Moss, and is very popular.)

We walk on with little Søndre to an old log cabin that many years ago was used to store food and nowadays is half inhabited by families of large and small chickens, which Egil was given as birthday presents on his sixtieth and on his sixty-fifth birthday. I take another photograph of the serious-faced Søndre holding a splendid cockerel – it keeps surprisingly still – which is clearly one of the family. We go through the right-hand entrance of the log cabin, a white door with broad, slanting red panels, which form a decorative square in the middle. It seems to be a magic doorway; we do not know what will be waiting for us in the half-light on the other side. Up a creaking staircase, we reach the loft where Egil hoards more of his wooden treasures. And there, suddenly, are the colours, especially the red, that I am looking for to include in a picture that I want to take in the garden. Red-aproned little women and two small men with red Noddy caps, which at Christmas, each with a red lantern in their hands, illuminate the path in front of the house. We bring them out into the open air and set them up between the tree trunks that stand around a small Iron Age grave-mound covered with tall grass, a protected monument which stands at the end of the lawn. The shining red of these pixie men and women enlivens a mysterious gloomy space between this dense group of tree trunks, a horse chestnut in the centre and a few ash trees, one or two of which are already dead. The scene makes me think of Heinrich Böll's short story *Not only at Christmas* (*Nicht nur zur*

LEFT The wooden giraffe stands alert with tail high, as if startled by the flying geese.

ABOVE A raised store used as a chicken shed. Egil Gabrielsen's wood carvings are hoarded like treasures behind the closed door with the red squares like a magic pattern.

LEFT Contented cockerels and hens sun themselves or scratch at the earth among the bedding marigolds.

81

LEFT The Christmas figures, having an
unaccustomed airing, look a little out of
place in the bright summer light. But the
fresh red certainly enlivens the grey trunks
of the ashes around a small Iron Age
grave-mound and the green of the horse
chestnut in the middle of the grove.

RIGHT Red 'sails' surprise us in front of a
wooden wall, contrasting with the great
pinnate leaves of the wild parsnip, which
in Norwegian is called the 'tromsøpalme'
after the town of Tromsø in the far north,
where this decorative and almost tropically
luxuriant perennial grows and grows in the
midnight sun.

BELOW The same grove without the figures
and with just its lichen-covered tree
sculptures. In the background is the lawn
with the blue glass ball and the yellow-
ochre house. All over the garden are
secrets awaiting discovery, whether an
ancient burial mound or an animal taken
from a fable and carved by Egil Gabrielsen
for his grandson.

RIGHT Egil Gabrielsen's animal sculptures, which are often related to popular fables, have become well-loved in his locality.

BELOW The flowers of waterlilies (*Nymphaea alba*) close as evening shadows fall across the clear pond by the farm house, where once cows would come to drink.

BELOW The still green spherical flowers of globe thistles (*Echinops bannaticus*) – later they turn steel-blue – in a play of light and shade in front of the yellow wall of the house.

OPPOSITE Egil Gabrielsen's grandson Søndre sharing a private moment with the family's magnificent tame cockerel.

Weihnachtszeit), in which a woman develops a fixation about Christmas and celebrates Christmas Day every day of the week, even in the middle of summer, with Christmas tree, candles, her family and friends, and the vicar, until the guests have had enough of the whole business and increasingly find ways of absenting themselves. Egil Gabrielsen grins at the Christmas scene brought forward to July and takes me to see his modern and exciting wooden red sculpture, a triangle and a square in front of a dark wooden boundary wall. The red, discoloured by the rain, is half-covered by the large leaves of the wild parsnip with their deeply cut lobes, but shines intensely in the sunshine in front of the dark background. This plant (*Heracleum* sp.) grows everywhere in the north of the country and in Norwegian is called '*tromsøpalme*', after this town of the far North.

After this contrast of light and dark I am attracted by a very light scene: the green heads of a row of globe thistles (*Echinops bannaticus*) in front of the yellow wall of the house where there is light shade and patches of sunshine. It is the middle of July and in a few weeks the globes will stand out steel-blue against the ochre background. But now it is the turn of the vibrant yellow of the loosestrife, recurring in groups and in front of the wall of the house where the two yellows intermingle. A joyous atmosphere predominates, from the repetition of yellows and reds, and is enhanced by the colours of the chickens that strut about. Evening falls and the leaves of the ligularia gleam reddish-brown against the light in front of the pond, where once the cows from the old farm would gather to drink and where the white water lilies will soon be closing.

Following a warm and friendly farewell, I ring up the Gabrielsens from my house in Skåne in September, and then again from Genoa in November, when I am sad to learn that Egil Gabrielsen died on 31 October 1998. But the rural idyll remains, captured in my pictures: the white-and-black chickens in the marigold bed, or in front of their brown log cabin, the cockerels proudly stepping out between the red of the begonias and the yellow of the loosestrife; and the white birds brought alive by the wind, their wings whirling above the light dove-blue that leads us to the distance, just as long ago, Nils Holgersson, in the story *Tom Thumb*, was led at the outset of his long, miraculous journey with the wild geese.

Anna swings up above the wandering

hedges with their amber and gold leaves

until she flies high over the magic lake…

Seaside &
Lakeshore

ABOVE The terrace by the house, with children's play area.
BELOW Looking up the slope to the house: waves of green lawn
are contained by the two main curving beech hedges, which in
autumn are a tapestry of amber, gold and green.
OPPOSITE Separated from the main garden by a public footpath
is the lakeside garden with its landing stage: an enchanting
place where the wind rustles the reeds and the leaves.

Flowing Lawns & Beech Hedges

A grassy slope flows the length of the garden between curving beech hedges, its green waves corresponding with the ripples along the lake shore at the bottom. The hedges and lakeside trees glow with their most beautiful amber and gold autumn tints. The lake determines the far end of this delightful property in Silkeborg, in the middle of Jutland, which in addition to the main garden includes a further area of lake shore, separated from the public footpath by a white wooden fence and beech hedges. Here there is a lawn, and reeds, trees and a landing stage. In area the main garden consists of some 900 square metres (a little over 1000 square yards), and the lakeshore of some 280 square metres (335 square yards).

But let us return to the hedge garden on the slope. The landscape architect Torben Schønherr managed to get an abundance of spaces out of this small site for its then owners, Liselotte Hamann and Henning Sørensen and their young family (they have recently sold the property). The curving hedges running the length of the slope form the main lines of the garden, now widening, now narrowing the central lawn, and this gives a dynamic tension to the whole. Through opposite pairs of openings in the main hedges, we can enter a series of smaller spaces, three on the left and a further three on the right. These six side rooms are separated from each other by shorter beech hedges which run across the slope, and at an angle to it. They include a kitchen garden with herbs and a raised vegetable bed; a small garden with flowering perennials and summer flowers; a play area for the three children, who anyway have the free run of the garden for playing hide-and-seek behind the hedges; a fruit garden; a scented garden with jasmine growing into the hedges and even a woodland garden with wild berries.

At the time of planting, the hedge plants for the whole garden were just about half-a-metre (20 inches) tall, which meant that the costs could be kept down; it took some five years before the separate spaces began to develop a noticeable form. (When I took my photographs the hedges were eight years old.)

Little by little, by means of the curved lines of the hedges,

Silkeborg, Denmark

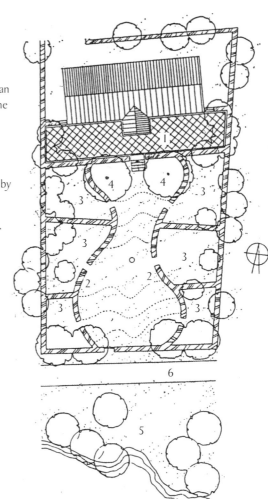

Torben Schønherr's plan of 'The girl lying on the lakeside'
1 terrace & play area
2 main beech hedges
3 smaller gardens on either side, separated by lower, straight beech hedges
4 the 'paradise apples' (now removed; two cherry trees were planted centrally)
5 lakeside garden
6 public footpath

ABOVE Looking up from the bottom of the slope we can understand the dynamic effect of the main hedges.
BELOW The lawn, spangled with leaves from the two cherry trees, curves towards the lake. Vertical tree trunks contrast with its undulating form, casting playful shadows.
BELOW RIGHT From the smaller side gardens, view across the garden through openings in the hedges to a curved bench.

the long slope was changed into a well-proportioned garden with a perspective. The hedges narrow down the central lawn area and then widen it out again. The clever division of the terrain produces not only rooms but also a sense of variety and security. Beech hedges are ideal as space dividers and also as curved sculptures, their autumn colours iridescent with yellowish-green changing to gold and amber.

The movement of the sinuous lines of the taller, flowing hedges is best observed from the balcony or terrace of the house. From here we can see why their wavy forms enclosing the curved spaces of the lawn are especially effective on sloping terrain. On the flat, the tension in the movement would be reduced because the sequence of the spaces could not be seen all at once. But starting from the bottom of the slope we can also register an interesting effect, as the hedges' linear form changes constantly the further up we climb. And if we go into one of the side garden rooms, we can see through openings across to the opposite room on the other side of the lawn. In so doing, we can also experience how these small spaces are set at slightly different angles to the slope.

But Torben Schønherr also wove poetry into his hedge art. If we look at his garden plan, we can – with a little imagination – see a rounded female torso. The gentle shaping of the terrain and the lines of the hedges have resulted in the form of a young woman, perhaps reclining. On the plan, planted on grass mounds where her breasts would be, two dwarf apple trees (*Malus sargentii*) are shown; significantly, with their abundance of white flowers in late spring and long-lasting dark red fruits, they are called 'paradise apples' in Danish. However, the family preferred to replace them with the taller sweet cherry trees, so that the children could have something to nibble while they played (they were planted at right angles to and between the apples on the plan). These changes to the trees and the grass outlines have over time flattened the girl's breasts: but garden art, though intact in the drawing, is by its nature ephemeral.

To accompany his plan Torben Schønherr wrote a poem entitled 'The girl lying on the lakeside', in which an old willow and a young girl are involved in a conversation. Early in the morning or late in the afternoon when the sun casts long shadows that give shape to the long lines of the beech hedges, we can indeed sense this girl, her green dress strewn with golden autumn leaves. We might also think of the stories of Hans Christian Andersen of the girl warming herself with matches, or of the little mermaid left behind on the shore by her brothers and sisters.

ABOVE Ripples on the lake framed by its little landing stage on one side and a pollarded willow on the other.

BELOW Early morning dew darkens the amber leaves on the lawn where the sun casts long shadows over the girl lying by the lake.

ABOVE Näs, home of Helena Emanuelsson and family. A circle of the pink rose 'Bonica' stands alone on the lawn. To the left is a glimpse of the old chestnut tree planted by great-grandmother Ester. OPPOSITE Alders and birches rise high above the long flower border, one end of which lies near the old wash-house.

RIGHT The garden, some two-and-a-half acres (a hectare) in size, forms part of surrounding parkland. Helena Emanuelsson's flower border is some 75 metres (250 feet) long and 7-10 metres (25-30 feet) wide.

1 yellow house
2 main house
3 circular rose bed
4 chestnut tree
5 the long border
6 summerhouse
7 old wash-house
8 fallen willow trunk
9 beach

Lakeside Flower Border

Helena Emanuelsson's flowers bloom close to a small lake. White blossoms and silver-grey foliage shine in the evening twilight, when other colours have already died away. When seen from a distance in strong daylight, the long broad ribbon border, with its shrubs, flowering perennials, wild flowers and grasses, is not very noticeable on the lakeshore. You have to go closer to discover its fine beauty.

The long flower bed runs along the edge of the lake for some 75 metres (250 feet), sometimes next to the reeds and in places right next to the water. It lies in the half-shade of alders and birches between a rust-red wash-house, once used for drying hops, and a soft creamy-yellow and turquoise-blue summer-house constructed in the 1930s. It adds a beautiful flourish to this lakeside garden, with its many fruit trees, its herb garden, greenhouse, rose garden and smaller flower beds. Näs, as this country estate in Östergötland is called, also contains woodland and agricultural land that is leased out.

Näs is home to Helena and Gunnar Emanuelsson and their three children, Ester, Alfred and Elin; their restored, yellow house is some two hundred years old. Henrik Jonsson and Catharina Fahnehjelm, the still active older generation of the family, live in the main white house that was built in 1850.

To begin my tour of the garden's long history, I walk with Helena across the large lawn, past a round rose-bed, to see great-grandmother Ester's chestnut tree, planted many years ago to protect house and home. This beautiful tree stands between the traditional country cottage garden and Helena's flower border on the shore of the small Lake Raklången. Years ago the ground there was marshy and waterlogged with nettles and dense vegetation. Helena's father, Henrik, gradually built up this vulnerable strip of land with stones gathered from the fields. He chose for it beautiful, strong alder trees, favouring especially those with trunks that grow in twos and threes. Helena wheeled up countless barrowfuls of earth, planted shrubs and, bit by bit, claimed virgin soil and added perennials. 'The planted flowers should blend in with nature,' she said. She

Tranås, Sweden

92

ABOVE Helena Emanuelsson wanted to create a flowering border among the trees on the lakeside, with lots of white flowers and silver-grey perennials that would shine out and still be visible from a distance in the evening twilight. Here, in early August are the silver-grey leaves and bright pink flowers of *Lychnis coronaria*, pink and white astrantias, scarlet astilbes, sidalcea, *Filipendula ulmaria* and white wisps of *Veronicastrum virginicum* 'Album'. Edging stones are not used to mark off the border from the lawn. There is just a strip of mown grass, which conceals a layer of newspaper to keep back the weeds.

'When I am no longer able to look after the plants,' says Helena, nature can reclaim the ground that I have borrowed from her. Then reeds and nettles will gradually reoccupy the area. Perhaps a few strong perennials will remain and show that there was once a human being here who had ideas. Gardening for me is a question of managing what my ancestors founded. That gives me fulfilment, but I don't want anyone to feel obliged to care for all this when I am no longer able to. Gardening ought to give pleasure and should never be done as a duty or under compulsion.'

That is a good piece of philosophy and the right attitude with such a large garden, which is her passion but demands work.

listed some forty species that already grew wild here, flowers such as marsh marigolds (*Caltha palustris*), meadow buttercups (*Ranunculus acris*), *Geum rivale*, purple loosestrife (*Lythrum salicaria*), yellow loosestrife (*Lysimachia vulgaris*), meadow-sweets (*Filipendula ulmaria*) and beautiful sedges such as *Carex*. But now let us look more closely at the planting of the lake-side flower bed.

There are large sections with silver-grey and greenish lamb's ears (*Stachys byzantium*), the light grey of different mugworts (*Artemisia*) and a multitude of white flower varieties throughout the year, such as *Astilbe*, *Dicentra eximia*, lilies and masterwort (*Astrantia*). Ideally placed here on the damp lakeshore are bistort (*Persicaria bistorta*) and meadowsweet (*Filipendula ulmaria*) which, with its one-and-a-half metres (5 feet) tall corymbs of creamy white flowers, harmonizes so well with the purple loosestrife and other shore perennials.

While white brightens the bed, grey tones soften the colours and bind them together. Helena composes her muted, light

ABOVE LEFT White-flowering astilbes, oxeye daisies and orange *Lilium* among meadowsweet (*Filipendula*), with *Persicaria wallichii* in the background.
RIGHT *Aconitum*, *Lysimachia vulgaris* and verbascum.
FOLLOWING PAGES: LEFT A path meanders along the centre of the bed between clumps of *Corydalis lutea*, *Lilium*, *Lychnis coronaria* and *Hosta sieboldiana*.
RIGHT Next to the lakeside, a large clump of *Hosta fortunei* 'Aureomarginata', with *Alchemilla mollis*, *Papaver orientale* and *Primula sieboldii*.

pictures in the border with these basic tones, which are repeated, but in changed shades, to form an overall rhythm. These are living, fleeting pastel compositions that fade away after a few days or weeks. Strong colours, such as red and orange, are used sparingly but deliberately. Amidst the white of the loose panicles of bistort and small marguerites and against the trunk of a birch tree, the red-orange of the lily 'Avignon' shines out as a powerful detail. A few steps farther and this scene links up with white 'Apollo' lilies, *Dicentra eximia* and lamb's ears with its pinkish little flowers, to form the brightest picture. Helena avoids annuals with loud colours in these light colour combinations. When we get closer, we can see how the monkshood (*Aconitum napellus*) teams up with a figwort, their stems and blue and yellow flowers intertwining. Helena held back from planting the fire-red Jerusalem cross (*Lychnis chalcedonica*) in the border until she thought of just the right place for it: in front of a light-barked birch. One composition is dark, almost gloomy, with the dark red of astilbe, purple astrantia and the dark purples of columbine (*Aquilegia*) and horned violet (*Viola cornuta*); a large patch of rose campion (*Lychnis coronaria*), with its fire-red little flowers on a greyish-white, matted hairy plant, provides a colourful balance in itself.

Against the light blue wash of the summer house, the sun falls on the light pink flowers of false mallow (*Sidalcea*), a white and a delicate pink-coloured astilbe and the creamy-white,

95

LEFT A light breeze ruffles the silver lake and tall reeds at its edge; their form is echoed by grasses in Helena Emanuelsson's border as it touches the shore. ABOVE The painted summer house makes a finale at one end of the border.

ABOVE Rings and troughs filled with sedums and other tiny plants stand near the opposite end of the border and its vaulted gateway, the fallen willow trunk. A clump of *Phalaris arundinacea* 'Picta' lies next to the old red wash-house.

long, airy blossoms of the meadowsweet which, like will-o'-the-wisps, stir in the gentle breeze under the alder trees. We arrive at a place where yellow-leaved varieties of spiraea, plantain lilies (*Hosta*) and marjoram (*Origanum*), with its bright blue flowers, contrast with forget-me-nots, baby blue-eyes (*Nemophila menziesii*) and the gentian-blue flowers of alkanet (*Anchusa azurea*).

'The garden should be full of small surprises, but you have to take time to discover them,' says Helena. The visitor wanders slowly on the narrow paths that criss-cross the flower border and discovers a marble egg in the bird's-nest-like centre of a Norway spruce (*Picea abies* 'Nidiformis'), a broken terracotta pot half overgrown with ivy, a cushion of moss, a blue glass ball that intensifies an area of blue flowers, and a wreath woven from plants taken from the wood.

At one end of the border, close to the rust-red wash-house, lies the horizontal trunk of a great willow that has been cut back; with its newly sprouted shoots it looks like a green gateway. Nearby a collection of tiny plants, species of stonecrop (*Sedum*) and dwarf cranesbill (*Geranium dalmaticum*) with its small, rich pink blossoms, is laid out in stone rings and troughs. The proximity of the lake continues to fascinate: the pink

torches of astilbe stand out against the reeds and the greenish-white, striped grass called gardeners' garters (*Phalaris arundinacea* 'Picta'), with its fine ear-like panicles of flowers is highlighted by the surface of the water.

At the other end of the border, a notable counterpoint to the flowing lines is provided by the creamy-yellow summer house, its doors and windows painted a refreshing turquoise. At the beginning of August strong, joyous colours predominate in the morning sunlight: the yellow of loosestrife (*Lysimachia punctata* and the wild *L. vulgaris*), the purple of rose campion (*Lychnis coronaria*) and the last pink foxgloves, now at the top of their stems, which are full of seed capsules. At the end of September the yellow of coneflowers (*Rudbeckia laciniata*) shines in front of the turquoise windows and a few metres further on, under a tall silver willow, the reddish-lilac-coloured autumn leaves of red-barked dogwood (*Cornus alba* 'Sibirica') are visible. A magnificent creamy-white hydrangea (*H. paniculata* 'Grandiflora') between the trees is an echo of the white flowers that have disappeared with the summer. From here we have the finest view of the water landscape of Raklången, and we take leave of Helena's beautiful, romantic garden on the shore of this small, hidden lake.

99

ABOVE The house perches at the highest point of the cliff, from where it commands a fine view of the sea and harbour, where yachts and dinghies come and go. OPPOSITE Beyond the garden wall lies open country of cliffs, with rock pools, shrubby plants and wild grasses looking out over a seascape spattered with small islands.

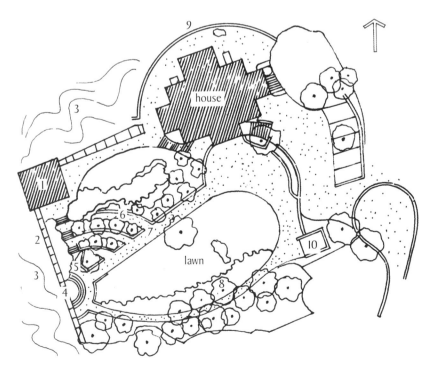

1 observation tower	5 steps to the tower	8 fruit trees
2 old high walls	6 terraces of roses,	9 new granite walls
3 wild cliff	fruit trees and bushes	10 tool shed
4 'Cyclopean' gateway	7 gravel slope	

Wind, Waves & Cliffs

Outside the high, hundred-year-old walls the wind and waves rule, and the cliffs with their wild grasses are proof against all weathers. At the very top, where two walls meet at right angles, a small square wooden observation tower slightly juts out to sea, perched above the rocks. Its timber sides are painted a pale creamy-yellow, beneath a white-painted, ornate fascia topped with a white railing. From the look-out platform on the roof, one can gaze out at the ever-changing sea or enjoy the view over the little harbour of Långedrag, home to the Royal Gothenburg Sailing Club (Göteborgs Kungliga Segelsälskap).

The design of the tower, which when seen from the garden resembles a cream-coloured pavilion, originates from the 1880s when Alfred Wennerlund, regional director of the Pripps brewery, had it built, at the same time as the house. But the ravages of time took their toll on its wooden structure, and so the new owners commissioned precise drawings to document the ruined watchtower before demolishing it and building an exact replica.

The garden, too, has been reconstructed. Before any work could begin, a mass of rubble and pieces of shattered rock, which had built up over the years, had to be removed. The slope was thus restored to its original dramatic contours and the slab of natural rock that rises up towards the watchtower and the little hollow that falls away gently towards an opening in the sea wall were once again brought to light.

Landscape architect Håkan Lundberg used grey granite to terrace the ground, measuring some 1700 square metres (almost half-an-acre), which was then planted with fruit trees and a herb garden. The ground at the bottom of the hollow, where a solitary horse chestnut survived from the original garden, has been laid with a lawn, and at its lowest part, a large group of rhododendrons and other evergreens, such as *Prunus laurocerasus* and *Ilex aquifolium*, thrive in the shelter of the

Långedrag, Göteborg, Sweden

ABOVE From a westerly direction, the view of the garden looks towards the yellow garden shed and a screen of tall trees above a dark wooden wall that shields neighbouring houses. Rock outcrops, planted with creeping stonecrops (*Sedum*) contrast with lawn and areas of longer grass, and in a small bed along the gravel path is the blue of delphiniums and the red of wild bleeding heart (*Dicentra eximia*). Young fruit trees, planted during the garden's complete redesign, stand before an ancient horse chestnut.

ABOVE The young fruit trees, terraces and rose-covered walls.
All the new stonework in the garden has been carried out in
the same grey granite, even the well-designed drainage
channel along the shallow steps of the gravel path.

ABOVE Outside the sea wall a steep gravel path with granite steps leads down to the sea from the opening in the garden wall, which is obscured by a white-blossomed elder.
BELOW The opening in the sea wall looks out across the ocean, like a Cyclopean arch from ancient Crete, with its great granite masonry blocks. The stones and pavings, made of the same granite, retain the sun's warmth.

ABOVE A flight of lighter granite-edged steps leads from the watchtower to a classical 'apse' dramatizing the opening in the sea wall. A red rose, 'Sympathie', lights up the foreground.
RIGHT Rocks above the terraced garden have earth pockets planted with various types of *Sedum* and *Sempervivum*, ideally suited to crevices such as these. The taller pink flowers belong to *Dicentra eximia*.

old wall. Where the wall reaches a height of about 7 metres (23 feet) a Cyclopean gate opens out towards the sea, its mighty granite stones glistening where they catch the sun. The mythical feel of this gateway is augmented by the classical lines of the semicircular stone steps leading from it into the garden. A steep stairway continues to the watchtower, and a gentler slope leads to a gravel area in front of the house. In between are small terraces where apple and pear trees thrive and cherries and plums ripen. Here and there the newly-built walls are clothed in climbing roses, but most striking of all are redcurrants glinting in the sun like fine rubies against the grey granite.

Beyond the sea wall, the property extends over cliff and rock: wild nature and landscape on the seashore, where the yellow grasses and pale red of dock (*Rumex*) and the scarlet berries of the red-berried elder (*Sambucus racemosa*) entice us; later in the summer, heather will be in blossom. Broad steps lead down from the Cyclopean gateway to the family's landing stage, and from here the wall with its observation tower seems to be higher than it really is, a symbol of a division between two worlds.

ABOVE The living gateway to Rungstedlund, like a relic of wall, is all that is left of an old whitethorn hedge that ran along the boundary of the property and 'Strandvejen', the old coast road between Copenhagen and Helsingør.

OPPOSITE The poet Johannes Ewald (see page 110) dedicated one of his most beautiful poems to Rungstedlund and in doing so presented the Danes with the ecstatic word 'lyksalighed'. It sounds like the German word 'Glückseligkeit' and has the same meaning of bliss or happiness. Ewald took a sad farewell from Rungstedlund, but something of this poet, whose steps Karen Blixen thought she heard in the house and whose thin figure she thought she saw on the meadow, lingers on in the atmosphere of the place.

©Sven-Ingvar Andersson

1 whitethorn gateway
2 shore road
3 courtyard
4 the pond
5 the white bridge
6 horse chestnut trees

7 former kitchen garden
8 orchard & site of new annual beds
9 Ewald's hill
10 Karen Blixen's grave

Karen Blixen's 'Place of Bliss'

One beautiful June morning in 1981, I walked for the first time under the green whitethorn gateway into the world of soft air and dancing light that was Karen Blixen's home. The chirping of birds and the scent of roses accompanied me into the courtyard of the L-shaped manorial house. Caroline Carlsen, faithful housekeeper to the internationally renowned writer, was waiting for me together with journalist Aase Holm, who had invited me to take photographs for a joint article. Madame Carlsen, as she is called, a small, elderly and friendly lady, had been at Rungstedlund since 1949; Karen Blixen had arranged for her to go on living there for as long as she wanted.

Madame Carlsen had arranged flowers in the rooms just as her mistress would have done during her lifetime. In a room that was as green as a moss-covered grotto were cut-glass vases of scented, cream-white roses. Called 'Gruss an Aachen' ('Greetings to Aachen'), this was an early scented Polyanthus rose, dated 1909, from the German rose grower Geduldig; it still flowers in the garden. The Green Room has a single, west-facing outer wall and is the warmest of all the rooms; Karen Blixen worked here in the cold season and took her afternoon tea in front of the wood fire. Now, the early summer morning streamed in through fine, transparent white curtains trimmed with lace; they trailed lightly on the floor in the slight breeze from an open window. Beyond, the landscaped garden beckoned: a picturesque backcloth of trees, a white bridge, an ancient and bizarre giant elder and a few tall ash trees are reflected in a pond, forming a romantic scene. The bridge leads over a small water channel which disappears into a fairy wilderness; beside the pond and channel is a luxuriant growth of butter burr, its big-toothed foliage forming a leafy roof to shelter an ugly duckling. It is the rare variety *Petasites albus* with white flowers, which are borne before the leaves in March and April; here, with thousands of spring snowflakes (*Leucojum*

Rungstedlund, Denmark

ABOVE & OPPOSITE The landscape architect Andreas Bruun devised an intriguing solution for his design for eight new annual beds in the old fruit garden, by placing them diagonally. Their lengths differ, but each is 4.5 metres (15 feet) wide and has a path of discreet cement-grey paving stones. The paths appear as long, pale shadows that sometimes almost disappear under the dense blue of catmint (*Nepeta* x *faassenii*), and sometimes bind the flowing blossoms of the summer flowers like a graphic frame. Two-metre (6-foot) wide grass paths surround the beds as a green background against which poppies (*Papaver somniferum*) stand out clearly.

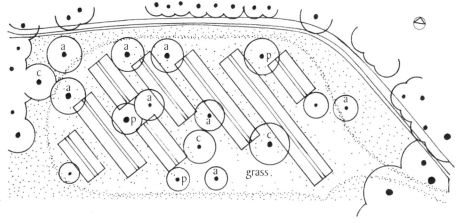

ABOVE The orchard area with its diagonally set flower beds, containing annuals that Karen Blixen would herself have used for cut flowers for the house. Fruit trees include: a = apple trees   p = pear trees   c = cherry trees

vernum), it announces the coming of spring.

On that first visit Rungstedlund seemed to me to be sleeping the sleep of Sleeping Beauty and seventeen years passed before I came again. Now, the whole house contains the Karen Blixen Museum and was opened to the public on 14 May 1991. After the filming of *Out of Africa*, people started to come here from all over the world. In June 1998, the museum's director, Marianne Wirenfeldt Asmussen, received me in the beautiful café. I was surprised at the changes, carried out to the west wing by Vilhelm Wohlert, one of the architects of the Louisiana Museum of Modern Art. The new, bright rooms were full of happy people, all wanting to learn more about Karen Blixen's work and life, and activities at Rungstedlund.

The garden had also changed in part since my previous visit. There are new planting areas in the perennial beds in the west garden, on both sides of the hornbeam hedge boundaries facing the house and terrace; a large, round bed at the end of the hedges contains the white rose 'Karen Blixen', raised by Poulsen nurseries and framed here with lavender. To the west of the pond, a new garden has beds for annual flowers supplying cut flowers for the house and also herbs for the kitchen. It is integrated into an old fruit garden to a design by the landscape architect Andreas Bruun (see page 147).

In a radio talk Karen Blixen gave in 1958, she announced the setting up of the Rungstedlund Foundation and described her home as follows: 'Rungstedlund comprises about forty acres of gardens, woods and meadows, all of which – among the well-kept gardens of the shore road – seems something like a wilderness. Around the pond and the canal in the garden there is a whole wood of the same sort of broad-leaved dock that Hans Christian Andersen's "happy family" lived beneath. There is a large peaceful field, protected from the wind, where horses and cows wander about. There are many old trees and under them a particularly rich woodland floor with anemones, primroses, and violets. In a corner to the northwest, towards which the entire property rises, lies Ewald's Hill.'

Here, under a large beech tree, is the site of Karen Blixen's grave (she died in 1962), where a casket of earth that she had brought home from Africa was scattered over her coffin. Every day, there are a few freshly picked wild flowers on her grave.

Karen Blixen's love of birds was inherited from her father; they find a paradise at Rungstedlund. Wilhelm Dinesen liked to go hunting and wrote a number of books, including his now classic *Hunting Letters* in two volumes. In her famous radio talk she went on to say: 'I was ten years old when my father died. His

THE HISTORY OF RUNGSTEDLUND

Some four hundred years ago the house was the oldest inn in the fishing village of Rungsted, between Helsingør and Copenhagen, where tired travellers liked to stop off. Young Johannes Ewald, who was to become one of Denmark's greatest poets, lived here during 1773–75. He suffered from arthritis and drank excessively, and his family left him in the care of the inn's owners, the Jacobsen family, away from the temptations of Copenhagen but, of course, too close to the bar counter. Here Ewald made friends among the local fishermen, farmers and sailors and wrote one of his most beautiful poems, 'Rungsted's Lyksaligheder' ('The Bliss of Rungsted'), and experienced 'the midsummer of his life'.

A century later, in 1879, Karen Blixen's father, Wilhelm Dinesen, and his sister Alvide bought a large property to the north of Copenhagen. It included four estates, one of which was Rungstedlund, the least grand of the four, but full of poetry and with an incomparable view across the Oresund. In 1881 Wilhelm Dinesen married Ingeborg Westenholz and they chose as their home Rungstedlund, a grand manorial farmhouse, now extended to all four points of the compass. In the following eleven years, three daughters, Inger, Karen (1885) and Ellen, and two sons, Thomas and Anders, came into the world. Sad years followed with the suicide of the much-loved father in 1895, probably because of an incurable illness, and three years later a devastating fire destroyed the east and south wings.

In 1914 Karen Dinesen married the Swedish Baron Bror von Blixen-Finecke and in the same year the couple emigrated to Kenya, where the Baron bought a coffee farm with the monies of both their families. In 1921 their marriage ended in divorce, but Karen Blixen carried on with the farm until 1931 when she returned ruined to Denmark and lived again at Rungstedlund. It was here, sitting at her father's desk in the east-facing 'Ewald's Room' with its sea view, where she liked to sit most of all, that she wrote her first book, *Seven Gothic Tales*; it soon became an international success. She wrote in English and Danish throughout her writing career and most of her other books were written at Rungstedlund, where after the death of her mother in 1939 she became the lady of the house. The Rungstedlund Foundation came into being in 1958 through the donation of the property by Karen Blixen and her brothers and sisters; it is also the seat of the Danish Academy of Literature. The royalties from her books were given in perpetuity to the Foundation and the garden and woodland were declared a bird sanctuary. Since then Rungstedlund has been in the care of a number of experts – ornithologists, ecologists, foresters, gardeners, architects, historians and writers – but abiding by Karen Blixen's last will and testament. Respect for her wishes has generally guided the development and care of the landscape and the garden.

KAREN BLIXEN'S FLOWERS

Less well-known than her books are Karen Blixen's poetic flower arrangements which always delighted her guests. This task sometimes took days and she spared herself no trouble; if some detail or other were missing, she would undertake excursions by bicycle to the gardens of friends. Steen Eiler Rasmussen, sometime Professor of Architecture at the Royal Academy of Art in Copenhagen and neighbour and counsellor of Karen Blixen, would often come to photograph her most subtle bouquets, usually on the day after her visitors departed. In his contribution to the book *Karen Blixen's Flowers*, he wrote: 'The arrangements could be as varied in character as her fantastic tales. They ranged from the large, robust, sumptuous selection that burgeoned in the wide tureen, opulent old-fashioned roses accompanied by red cabbage leaves, to the infinitely restrained arrangements of a few delicate flowers in a long-necked vase. To discuss which would take the prize would be foolish. Each was a finished composition....I can remember a unique bouquet...impressionistic, in green and white, composed of wild plants no garden artist would accept. It included the airy globes of dandelion 'clocks', carried indoors with incredible care, the white inflorescence of wild chervil with its lacy foliage, and finally something not immediately recognizable – namely sprays and twigs from the lime tree, stripped of all the leaves but with the wings of the flowers retained. The whole piece was a work of art that lasted for just one day. One draught through the large room and the white, downy fluff of the beautiful dream had quietly drifted away.'

Lisbeth Hertel, horticulturist and translator, highlights in her contribution to the book the way in which Karen Blixen, with her wide knowledge of cultural history, united the best elements of Danish tradition with those of other countries, particularly England: 'As with Hans Christian Andersen, there was also that added ingredient which the artist seems to call straight down from heaven.' And writing about tulips: 'Caroline Carlsen remembers that Karen Blixen sometimes bought tulips but they had to be...in full bloom, of the kind flower shops like to get off their hands while they are still saleable. Tulips are irritating flowers to arrange....Even if they are attractive to begin with, they only reach their full beauty, acquire "soul", after several days in a warm room. All the great flower painters knew that tulips are flowers with a will of their own....As I see it, her way of cutting through the "tulip problem" was a parallel to those greater matters: she stripped off the leaves – no nonsense. Everyone who has arranged tulips has taken off a limp leaf here and there, but I have never seen it done so consistently, with a complete fresh aesthetic effect...when her hands had finished with them, they were more than tulips. They had come to represent the idea of tulip.'

ABOVE One of the many nesting boxes in the grounds

ABOVE Silver wool: lamb's ears, *Stachys byzantina*.

ABOVE Alliums and BELOW honesty, *Lunaria annua*

death was for me a great sorrow, of a kind which probably only children feel. I think I was his favourite child and I know he thought I resembled him. He took me with him when he walked over the fields, when he troated for a roebuck in the woods, or searched through the marsh for snipe with his two French griffon hounds, Osceola and Matchitabano…named for two old Indian chiefs who were among his friends. I remember clearly how he taught me to distinguish among the various kinds of birds and told me about migratory birds, and his quick, happy reaction at the sight of a rare bird, the kite with a notched tail, like other people's happiness over a glass of good wine.'

The memory of the poet Ewald is something which Karen Blixen assimilated in literary terms and also gave expression to in the landscape garden, keeping it alive and even strengthening it. The wonderful view to the east to the wide expanses of the sea has remained, even though the forest of masts from the sailing boats in the small harbour is a pointer to our own times. From the house the tranquil perspective to the west with the lawns, the pond, the white bridge, the enchanted giant elder and tall ash trees, with the meadow, the grove of trees and sky, leads us back to paintings of the first decades of the eighteenth century, to pictures for example by Jean-Antoine Watteau with his enormous trees in arcadian groves and distant dancing vistas. Some fifty years later, in 1773, Johannes Ewald came to Rungstedlund and this perspective, as a retrospective view of the past age in which Ewald lived, is merely a product of chance.

The landscape architect Sven-Ingvar Andersson (see pages 14–19), points out in his contribution to *Karen Blixen's Flowers*, 'The Lost Paradise', that it was not until 1956 when one of the big horse chestnuts west of the lake had fallen down and a long vista had been opened up (it had previously only been partially visible in the winter) that Karen Blixen decided to make use of the potential of this new view to develop a garden space from the house to the grove that would indicate a gradual transition from cultivated to wild nature. Andersson goes on to observe the romantic scene on the pond, where he compares the picturesque elder tree with its finely branching twigs against the sky with rococo ornamentation: 'The garden of the Romantics was not merely a flight from reality, it was also a return to values and conditions which it was felt had been lost in the unemotional climate of rationalism….In the romantic garden people cultivated the lost paradise, and did so with energetic resignation. It is a paradox, but no doubt the sort of paradox Karen Blixen could understand and a situation with which she could identify.'

Yet Karen Blixen's vision of landscape also depended on the memory of her father Wilhelm Dinesen. He had spent three years in the wilderness living with the Indians of North America, without seeing a white man. He made friends with Indian chiefs and gave his income as a fur trapper to the 'red skins'. In 1854 Chief Seattle (Sealth), a native American mystic, gave a famous speech, 'This Precious Earth', when the Unites States was eager to buy 'his' land. Whether or not Karen Blixen was acquainted with it, this extract closes my circle around Rungstedlund:

'The Great Chief in Washington sends word that he wishes to buy our land. The Great Chief also sends us words of friendship and good will. This is kind of him, since we know he has little need of our friendship in return. But we will consider your offer. For we know that if we do not sell, the white man may come with guns and take our land. How can you buy or sell the sky, the warmth of the land? This idea is strange to us. If we do not own the freshness of the air and the sparkle of the water, how can you buy them? Every part of this earth is sacred to my people….The earth does not belong to human beings; human beings belong to the earth. This we know. All things are connected like the blood which unites one family. All things are connected….There is no quiet in the white man's cities. No place to hear the unfurling of leaves in the spring or the rustle of insects' wings. But perhaps it is because I am a savage and do not understand. The clatter only seems to insult the ears. And what is there to life if we cannot hear the lonely cry of the whipoorwill or the arguments of the frogs around a pond at night? I am a red man and do not understand. The Indian prefers the soft sound of the wind darting over the face of a pond, and the smell of the wind itself, cleansed by a midday rain or scented with the pinion pine. The air is precious to the red people, for all things share the same breath – the beast, the tree, the human, they all share the same breath….Our God is the same God. This earth is precious to God. Even the white people cannot be exempt from the common destiny. We may be brothers and sisters after all. We shall see….

The perfumed flowers are our sisters;
the deer, the horse, the great eagle,
these are our brothers.
The rocky crests, the juices of the meadows,
the body heat of the pony, and human beings –
all belong to the same family.'

ABOVE Among the native plants and grasses of the seashore
others found in the wild have been planted: here purple spikes
of 'Blåeld' or 'blue fire', otherwise viper's bugloss (*Echium
vulgare*), and sea thrift (*Armeria maritima*); and BELOW a bright
wave of Flanders' poppies. OPPOSITE For much of its course,
the little river is contained within pipes but just before it joins
the sea, Helge Lundström's rock garden has restored its dignity.

Seashore Rock Garden

Where the small river Nöbbelöv flows into the Baltic in south-eastern Sweden, there has for some years been a rock garden worthy of our admiration, for it blends most harmoniously with the fine coastal landscape of Österlen. Here on the road through the former fishing village of Brantevik, south of the picturesque little harbour town of Simrishamn, the garden designer and painter Helge Lundström has constructed various terraces along the river bed using local hard Cambrian sandstone. In among these terraces he has provided niches for plants, where in the summer the pale blue of viper's bugloss (*Echium vulgare*) mixes with the red of the Flanders' poppy (*Papaver rhoeas*). Here also, close to the beach, tourists and local people can find benches and tables for picnicking and somewhere to park their cars.

Helge, a well-known artist who has a great love for his local area, had long wanted to provide a more beautiful outflow to the sea for this small river. It rises as a spring in Östra Nöbbelöv and since the 1960s has largely been piped; here by the sea shore it re-emerges into the open. His plans included the creation of a play area for children, somewhere for them to jump, climb and splash in the water. This practical project was at last realized in the mid-1990s, thanks to the help of Kjell Nilsson, the owner of a local transport firm (who still provides a man for the upkeep of the park), and the good sense of Simrishamn local council.

The great blocks of stone come from Brantevik itself, where blasting was being carried out for the building sites of new housing projects. Formed ninety million years ago, this Cambrian sandstone is white but also has a light golden-brown colouring, a consequence of its different layers mixing with various minerals such as iron oxide. The stone's discreet patina helps the park blend into its seashore setting; it looks soft and warm even in the gleaming sunshine.

Prior to the artistic shaping of the park, the terrain, some

Brantevik, near Simrishamn, Sweden

LEFT Wild plants, including grasses and white cow parsley (*Anthriscus sylvestris*), are tucked into nooks and crannies among the rocks.

RIGHT From where it emerges near the village of Brantevik and its new houses, the river Nöbbelöv flows clear and fresh into the Baltic Sea.

700 square metres (7500 square feet) in size, was prepared and shaped with machines, and additional, thin, sandy earth was spread. By chance it also contained the seeds of the red Flanders' poppies which now display their powerful colour. Under the direction of Helge Lundström, four men completed the work within one week. To achieve this, the artist selected the stones before transportation and then at the outset positioned the biggest and most sculptured boulders here and there as leitmotifs. Gradually a context for the stones was built up until the picture was finished, and the area became a small, landscaped seashore garden.

The plants in this rock garden of stone monoliths along the riverbank and adjoining terrain naturally had their role to play. On the shore, the wild vegetation consists partly of marram grass (*Ammophila arenaria*), a plant that anchors itself in the sand with an underground network of stems and builds up dunes; there is also grey-green mugwort (*Artemisia vulgaris*), cow parsley (*Anthriscus sylvestris*) with its umbels of white flowers and the half-metre (20-inch) tall, pale blue flower spikes of viper's bugloss (*Echium vulgare*), which in Swedish is called '*Blåeld*' ('blue fire'). To complement these plants, Helge

Lundström planted the local yellow-flowering yellow flag (*Iris pseudacorus*), mugwort (*Seriphidium maritimum*), the grass-like clumps and carnation-like crimson flowers of sea thrift (*Armeria maritima*), speedwell (*Veronica longifolia*) with its erect racemes of blue flowers nearly a metre (3 feet) long and sea kale (*Crambe maritima*), with its thick, pinnate, blue-grey foliage and small white flowers in dense racemes.

As a garden designer, Helge Lundström has designed numerous private and public gardens using natural stone and plants all over Sweden: one example is the impressive garden in the old Malmö castle park opposite the municipal library. He lives in Gislöv, also in Österlen, in a picturesque house some three hundred years old with a small garden full of the charm of rich and rare plants.

Opposite his garden, across the lane, is his rose-covered studio with its beds of exquisite perennials that are admired by passers-by, and blocks of natural stone in non-traditional sculptural forms. Working with the stones and uncovering their veins increasingly absorbs him and gives his life its fulfilment, but when he takes time off from this pursuit, he paints and draws the beautiful, subtle landscapes of his locality.

Edvard Grieg's 'Hill of the Trolls'

It was the music of Edvard Grieg, which I love so much, that brought me to Hop, south of Bergen, and this path through a small wood. It is lined by ancient, crooked beech trees, each with its bizarre shape, like an enchanted being, drawing me onwards to the fateful Troldhaugen, the hill of the Trolls, where in 1885 Edvard Grieg and his wife Nina moved into their newly built villa. The path climbs up for a short while until one catches sight of the fascinating creamy-white wooden house with its slanting slate roofs rising up at different angles and levels, its pointed gables and handsome balcony. The architecture of its turreted rear view dates from the age of eclecticism, when stylistic elements were borrowed both from the Continent and from England; here it adopts rectangular forms so that the vertical observation tower harmonizes with the richly decorated, protruding glass veranda on the ground floor.

The veranda doors open to discharge a swarm of visitors from the world over, and there is Eilif B. Lötveit coming towards me, dark-haired, bespectacled and with a wry smile. This fortunate man, a native of Bergen, is the museum's concert manager and administrator; it is he who makes Grieg's rich œuvre available to music-lovers around the globe, who derive such pleasure from it. Lötveit, who studied literature, Scandinavian languages and German culture, requests that I speak German with him. A man of wit and humour, he enjoys speaking my mother tongue and speaks it well, and I listen happily to his stories about the life of Edvard Grieg. We go inside where visitors can see the composer's battered suitcase, trophies and silk ribbons along with mementoes of his many guest concerts abroad. There are some of his original manuscripts, various curios, the masterly portraits by Erik Werenskiold and finally the Steinway grand piano in the living room. This was a present from the music lovers of Bergen on the occasion of Edvard and Nina Grieg's silver wedding, and today it aptly continues to give pleasure to concert audiences.

A steep, narrow path, lined with ferns and the bizarre stems of ancient rhododendrons, leads down to the beautiful lake, past a discreet piece of modern architecture constructed in concrete and wood and integrated with its rock surroundings. It is the new concert hall, probably the only one in the world with a grass roof. The dark red composer's cabin stands farther down on the lake shore. It has just one window facing the lake and when there is no sun the interior is quite dark. In sunlight, the shadowy room changes into a poetic space and the desk in front of the window comes alive again, with its ink well and other small utensils, just as when Edvard Grieg composed there.

ABOVE The front (left) and rear views of Troldhaugen, a few miles to the south of Bergen, which was Grieg's home from 1885 until his death in 1907. RIGHT Lake Nordåsvannet glimpsed through the trees. Ferns flourish in the shade of a tall ash tree and pale lichen shines on moss-covered rock.

Hop, near Bergen, Norway

ABOVE One of the massive beech trees with remarkable shapes that rise by the path at the approach to Troldhaugen. Like a musical overture, they anticipate and heighten the visitor's excitement in arriving at the house of the great composer.

ABOVE An old moss-covered rhododendron and a jungle of ferns are evidence of the
prevailing damp climate here – fine for bringing on plants but not so beneficial for the
composer who suffered constant ill-health, partly as a result of living here.

HISTORY & MUSIC

The Griegs had been married for eighteen years before they found their summer refuge at Troldhaugen. It was an otherwise restless life spent making countless journeys between Europe's music capitals, for there has been scarcely another composer and conductor so celebrated and beloved in his own lifetime as Grieg was. Nina Grieg accompanied him on these journeys; she herself was an acclaimed singer and the best interpreter of her husband's 'romances'. In April 1885 the Griegs moved into their beautiful new villa. Edvard Grieg's cousin, the architect Schak Bull, had helped them with its construction. Inside are bare wooden walls, like those still seen today in old Norwegian farmhouses. From the outside the house is *mondaine*, that of a sophisticate; inside it has the warmth of wood matured in its Norwegian homeland: such ambivalence occurs in Grieg's life itself.

What Troldhaugen meant to Grieg becomes clear from a letter dated mid-March 1885 and written to his publisher, Dr Max Abraham of Edition Peters in Leipzig: 'During these days I really do not know whether I am a musician or a builder. Every day I take the train out to the villa and back again. All my ideas get used up there and unborn works are swallowed up *en masse* by the earth. When you come to see us, you need only to dig and Norwegian choral, orchestral and piano pieces will come gushing out of the earth! That they look like peas and potatoes and radishes need not confuse us, for there really is music in them.'

Grieg had started his musical studies aged fifteen, in 1858, at the famous Leipzig Conservatory; he took his finals there in 1862. His examiners noted that he possessed 'very notable musical talent especially in composition'. Leipzig, with its Conservatory founded by Felix Mendelssohn-Bartholdy in 1843 and with the progressive and open mind of Robert Schumann, acted as a magnet to the musical world. The classical romantic style flourished and young German and Scandinavian composers mutually inspired each other. A musical renewal followed, with Niels W. Gade and his first symphony and Edvard Grieg's poetic contribution of songs and piano pieces, created with his fine sense for elaborate acoustic nuance. Before Grieg moved into Troldhaugen, he had already composed his piano concerto, the incidental music to 'Per Gynt', the string quartet in G Minor, his first two violin sonatas, the Holberg Suite as well as the great piano works, the Sonata in E Minor and the Ballad in G Minor. It was, especially, works of an intimate format that would be written in Troldhaugen. However, besides the many smaller pieces for the piano and the 'romances', it was also in Troldhaugen at the turn of the year 1886–87 that he composed one of his greatest masterpieces, the Violin Sonata in C Minor. Later came a series of lyrical pieces for the piano, and probably also 'Haugtussa' (the child from the mountains), the song cycle for Arne Garborg's poems.

OPPOSITE & RIGHT Grieg had the composer's cabin built in 1892, describing it as 'my little workshop, from which I expect so much'. Yet it is doubtful whether, given his precarious state of health, it brought him the expected happiness. At first the cabin was only poorly insulated and Grieg, who had had a lung problem since his youth, began to suffer from gout, perhaps as a result of draughts and damp. On the chair in front of the old, black piano is a heavy book, placed there to raise the height of the seat. That is how the physically small composer was able to reach the keyboard – on a doubly secure musical base, for the book is an old edition of Beethoven's 32 piano sonatas edited by Grieg's teacher Ignaz Moscheles.

OPPOSITE BELOW The new concert hall with its roof of flowering grasses and delicate white blooms.

During a fruitful period of work Grieg wrote to a friend: 'Troldhaugen seems more beautiful to me every morning.... And the wonderful peace and quiet for getting on with work here once all the visitors have left. I scarcely dare tell you how splendid it is now. You know these tranquil autumn days full of wonderful colours, they hold quiet and yet more quiet....'

However, over the years the damp, west Norwegian climate undermined Grieg's health. (He was ill throughout his life, and visited sanatoria at home and abroad.) More than once he was tempted to sell Troldhaugen and settle in Kristiania, present-day Oslo. In one of his last diaries he wrote:

'No, Troldhaugen…is a love for which I am paying a high price, it is taking my life! But west Norway also gave me life, the enthusiasm for life, the goal of setting it to music. If I could only risk the step of tearing myself away…and spending the rest of my life in a dry climate which is essential for me. But I haven't the heart to do it!'

The degree to which Grieg, the great European, was inspired by his home area of Bergen time and again is clearly demonstrated in the speech he gave on his sixtieth birthday on 15 June 1903:

'It is not only the art and science of Bergen that I have drawn my strength from….No, the whole atmosphere of Bergen, its milieu that enfolds me has served as my material. The smell at the German Quay (*Tyskebryggen*) still fills me with enthusiasm, indeed I even think that there is codfish in my music.'

His fine feeling for atmosphere is also mirrored in his letters and writing. In his 1865 diary for example, the twenty-two-year-old Grieg describes his impressions on a journey to Italy so vividly that the light, the air and the scents become almost palpable.

Local popular music is also part of the atmosphere of the mountains of west Norway that he loved so much. Grieg enjoyed listening to the brilliant local country singers and the musicians playing on the Hardanger fiddle (the Hardanger fjord is situated in Hordaland county in west Norway), a richly decorated fiddle with four melody strings and four resonating strings. Grieg encouraged gifted practitioners of Norwegian popular country music and incorporated this unspoilt original music with sounds from nature and mountain melodies into the flow of his own poetry-filled art. Amongst other pieces he also arranged seventeen 'Slåtter' (Peasant Dances), originally played on the Hardanger fiddle, as Opus 72 for the piano.

After Grieg's death in 1907, the casket with his ashes was

ABOVE A life-size bronze statue of Grieg after an original by Ingebrigt Vik: small in height but great in stature, the composer appears to be listening to nature.
BELOW Like a giant caterpillar, a natural rock wall sculpted by nature glides along the gravel path above the lake and the composer's cabin.

placed in the rock face of a cliff on Lake Nordåsvannet, a wild and romantic spot which he had chosen himself. Nina Grieg survived her husband by a further twenty-eight years.

For the first years after Edvard's death, Troldhaugen remained Nina Grieg's summer holiday home and a meeting place for friends and musical pilgrims. With the coming of the First World War and the subsequent economic crisis, she had to sell the property in 1919 and the majority of the furniture went under the hammer for auction. Careworn and saddened by these events, she settled in Copenhagen. However, fortunately, it was Grieg's second cousin, Joachim Grieg, who purchased Troldhaugen, both the house and the gardens. In 1923 he made a gift of the property to the town council of Fana, on condition that it would be used in keeping with the spirit of Grieg and the traditions of his house. A committee under the leadership of Mrs Aslaug Mohr dedicated itself untiringly to finding and acquiring, piece by piece, the original furniture and fittings of Troldhaugen.

In 1928 the Grieg Museum of Troldhaugen was officially opened to the public. The first international Bergen Festival took place in 1953 and the programme included daily matinée concerts in Troldhaugen; the house holds audiences of up to ninety people. From 1957 onwards the Troldhaugen Museum has organized its own series of summer concerts.

The artist Erik Werenskiold painted Grieg in 1902 in the West Norwegian mountains. He depicted the composer in profile, wearing an elegant coat and hat just like a gentleman in the Paris or Berlin of that time, rather as he appears in the lifesize statue in the garden (left above). This impressionist painting with its red, brown and violet tints symbolizes the artist and man of the world whose clothing forms a strange contrast to the natural scenery around him. The contrast is even greater in a black and white photograph showing the portly painter in his informal rustic clothing in the process of painting the picture: the small, slender and elegant figure of Grieg stands a few metres away from the easel in the foreground, alone and almost lost amidst the chaotic mountain landscape. Werenskiold's painting shows the white-haired figure of Grieg, just five years before his death. It is a poetic image that unites Edvard Grieg – the genius of the composer and the mystery of the man – with the harmonious world of nature.

RIGHT Grieg's music springs from the countryside and especially the landscape around Troldhaugen with its pine trees and cliffs on the pale blue lake; on this July morning the scene is as harmonious as his musical compositions.

The small princess from Drottningholm

lingers among the flowers while she

awaits the homecoming of her favourite

white dove…

Town & Village

ABOVE & BELOW The garden's layout is a culmination of the work of leading landscape and garden designer C.Th. Sørensen. He used elliptical forms for many of his creations, and his inspiration for this garden came from his own daughter Sonja Poll, who owns the property.

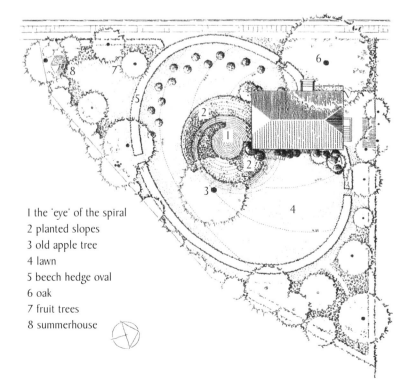

1 the 'eye' of the spiral
2 planted slopes
3 old apple tree
4 lawn
5 beech hedge oval
6 oak
7 fruit trees
8 summerhouse

Oval in a Triangle

From a sunken circular granite-paved terrace, the path spirals upwards and the area broadens out with each step we take, until we are standing on a lawn 2.5 metres (8 feet) above the terrace. A high beech hedge, taller than a man, takes up this dynamic spiral, making a broad curve around the picturesque apple tree and enfolding the cosy-looking house, to bring the elliptical movement to a gradual close. Visible as a bird's eye view on the plan of the garden, this masterly work of art can be grasped to the full. The sunken circle with the sloping ground and the curve of the path around it looks rather like a snail's shell. It forms, as it were, the negative image of a spiral shell, which was a favourite motif of the Baroque period; here, with the addition of the oval beech hedge, it creates a work of art for our own time. The design was created by Carl Theodor Sørensen (1899-1979), one of the great landscape architects of the twentieth century. The skilful way in which he dealt with the problem presented by the plot's difficult triangular shape, some 1200 square metres (a quarter-acre) in area, is best illustrated by the garden plan. The beech hedge allows the house to stand out, like a precious stone mounted in a ring. Its oval form, set on the slant, takes up more of the surface area than would a circle and all but touches the three boundaries of the site, so giving the largest possible enclosed, curved space.

Passageways between the beech oval and the boundaries connect the remaining parts of the garden, which contain a wild area with fruit trees and a summer house in one corner. The house has a generous approach in the form of a front garden with an oak tree, which gives pleasure to passers-by.

It is the interior of the garden, however, that holds our fascination, with its great snail-shell pattern. How you see it is up to you: either reposing within itself, crawling slowly along; or, like a flash, triggering off a spiral movement which is picked up by the oval movement of the curved beech hedge. Conversely, the dynamism of the hedges slowly gathers momentum and accelerates downwards like a whirlpool into the sunken spiral, to end in front of the blue glass doors.

C.Th. Sørensen, as his name is usually written in Denmark,

Holte, near Copenhagen

ABOVE The spiral path leads up and away from the sunken terrace in front of the blue basement doors, and sets off a dynamism that is caught and carried by the slope of the lawn and the oval form of the surrounding beech hedges. Flickers of morning light play over the ivy-covered shady bank, the paved path and the circular terrace. Strawberries grow on the sunnier bank to the right and in October the gnarled apple tree produces rosy-cheeked apples.

left this splendid garden design, his last piece of work, to his daughter Sonja Poll, now silver-haired and wearing her favourite colour blue. She could not have received a more beautiful birthday present. She followed in her father's footsteps as a landscape architect, and had given her father the inspiration for the sunken terrace. Although the oval beech hedge was planted in 1972, she was not able to begin carrying out the main part of his plan until 1980, a year after his death, when the 4-metre (12-foot) wide sunken terrace was laid out.

The earth from the excavation of the sloping pit was used to shape and level the lawn, which was to extend as uniformly as possible around the house. The old apple tree and the already established beech hedge determined the height of the garden area. Since the sunken terrace is so close to the house, every care had to be taken to provide an adequate drainage system to prevent the cellar flooding.

The two small but steep slopes either side of the house are planted with ivy on the shadier side and with wild strawberries on the sunny side. In summer the berries fruit frequently – to the delight of visiting children who enjoy picking and eating them. In spring the slopes are covered in crocuses, then with daffodils and grape hyacinths (*Muscari armeniacum*), with their

BELOW A blue bowl, filled with water for the birds, gleams among the ivy in the shade of the bank and by its shape and colour takes on a larger significance in the garden's vocabulary.

scented cobalt-blue flowers and whitish mouths. A dark blue, watery eye stares up from the bottom of the ivy-covered slope, caught by the morning sun as it shines through the crown of the gnarled apple tree and sends spots of light dancing across the dark green carpet. The glassy 'eye' is in fact a shallow ceramic bowl, placed there to refresh the garden's feathered visitors.

The lawn between the ancient apple tree and the hedge has deliberately been sparsely planted, because here colourful flower beds would only distract from the strong sculptural forms and lines. But on the west side, the lawn is enlivened with a few islands of flowering perennials, framed with paving stones. Each of the blossoms, such as monkshood (*Aconitum napellus*), masterwort (*Astrantia major*), black snake-root (*Cimicifuga racemosa*) and *Inula ensifolia* stands out clearly against the beech hedge foliage.

At an opening leading behind the hedge, Sonja makes a sweeping gesture towards the wild plants that are green and flowering under the fruit trees and laughs, 'Here anything goes'. This is a green world unto itself, a 'wilderness', where here and there a few ferns and flowering perennials grow, but where freedom, even chaos, rules, quite in contrast to the spartan lawn inside the oval. Behind the scenes, so to speak, where well-kept hedges and unkempt nature merge, is a place to take a rest: a necessary reverse side of the coin, which is also an essential part of the garden, with its ups and downs, dynamism and repose, light and shade.

We retrace our steps, absorbing the finer points of this work of garden art as we walk across the elliptical space formed by the 3-metre (10-foot) high beech hedge. We can only ever see one stretch of hedge at a time, of course, sometimes more curving, sometimes straighter, depending on where we are standing. The apple tree, like a mediator between the higher lawn area and the deeper circle of paving stones, stands close to the elliptical path, inside a section of hedge that runs almost straight. Close to the entrance, the oak tree shares a similar position against the hedge. So the bold forms of these two singular trees have the calmest of backdrops formed by the hedge; at the same time its horizontal line provides a strong contrast to the vertical trees. The dynamic effect of the elliptical hedge increases away from the trees and the house, to the east and the west, where very little else in the garden is 'happening'.

The form and thrust of the spiral is deeply anchored in nature. One who discovered its fascination and illustrated with great beauty some of the spiral tendencies of plants was Johann Wolfgang von Goethe (1749–1832). He saw that if the end of a

ABOVE & BELOW The lawn, shaped with earth dug from the terrace, flows out from the house as if in calm but perpetual motion. It is reined in by the great protective shape of the old apple tree which fills the space in the almost bare oval, mediating between the circular hollow and the sweeping beech hedge. An evergreen *Prunus laurocerasus* veils the corner of the house (to gain a firm foothold it was planted in a crate).

ABOVE The modest but welcoming house is barely visible from the street, being half hidden behind the beech hedge and screened by the stately oak. It is not until visitors step behind the house that they feel the drama of the highly charged beech hedge and the magical hollow of the terrace.

dandelion stem is cut open and both sides of its hollow tube are gently separated, each one rolls up and hangs like a pointed, spiral-shaped curl, to the delight of children – and adults – witnessing this entrancing natural event. In his exploration of the nature of growth, Goethe distinguished between a feeding spiral system and a supportive, upward-directed vertical system, two opposite forces which are mutually dependent. But the insights showed by Sørensen in his green geometry are also certainly rooted in nature, which is why their effect is so pleasing. He used the ellipse in numerous designs because its mathematical proportions have a similar harmony to Euclid's famous golden section. These include open air theatres and the wonderful garden colony in Naerum (see page 176). It was through C.Th. Sørensen's work with children in developing adventure playgrounds (see page 11) that I had the good fortune to meet this warm and easy-going man. Despite his fame he remained simple and unassuming and, with his charming wife Asta, regaled me with stories from his life that was fulfilled by his happy profession.

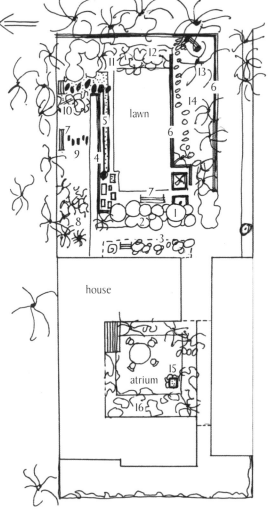

1 box spheres
2 ceramic bird
3 small box
shapes
4 yew hedge
5 water channel
6 hornbeam
hedge
7 bench
8 yellow border
9 purple border
10 Japanese
corner
11 Japanese maple
12 perennial
border
13 *Sorbus
americana*
14 shade garden
15 fountain
16 blue & yellow
border

Spheres, Parallels & Garden Rooms

Appealingly round, soft, fashioned spheres of box in varying sizes – small, large and increasingly gigantic – flank a brown-brick area leading off the entrance path to Eva and Bertil Hansson's house. The precise white pointing of the dark brick house is just visible shining through the almost tropical lush green and white suspended ornaments of a climbing hydrangea in flower. The dynamic, radiant forms of part-free and part-tamed vegetation contrast with the clear, almost severe, lines of the architecture, arousing curiosity for the main garden behind the hedges.

The planning of the tall hedges was the starting point for Bertil Hansson's laying out of the garden in 1970. The site, with the house and a small atrium, barely 800 square metres (1000 square yards) in size, is situated in a densely developed estate, where the flat landscape is often exposed to strong winds. The tautly-cut hornbeam hedges not only give protection from the elements, but also divide the main garden in front of the house, which is just 400 square metres (480 square yards), into individual spaces. These are clearly seen from an upper window.

The right-hand side of the narrow lawn is framed by a hornbeam hedge that does not close the lawn off from the garden, however. This hedge lies parallel to a second hornbeam hedge on the perimeter of the garden; in between is a space for plants that like shade. Along the left-hand side of the lawn runs a yew hedge, half the height of the other hedges and accompanied at a little distance from it by a water channel.

Although the straight division of this small garden to create spaces emphasizes its rectangular shape, the massive round box shapes, some smaller picturesque trees and bushes and the ample planting of soft, luxuriantly flowering perennials provide essential contrasts. We are reminded of the intimate enclosures characteristic of earlier twentieth-century gardens such as Hidcote and Sissinghurst; Bertil Hansson has indeed been influenced by these gardens, by books on the subject and visits to England, but also by an uncle's garden in Helsingborg. He grew to love this garden where as a boy he spent happy times,

Lund, Sweden

OPPOSITE ABOVE A jumble of box balls in a variety of sizes and other geometrical figures line the path and brick paving by the house. A climbing white hydrangea smothers the walls with, in the foreground, a white clematis (*C. potaninii* var. *fargesii*) and a pot with a haze of purple annual lobelia.

ABOVE Sensual forms that give a feeling of harmony: the Hansson family can observe the scenery surrounding a watchful bird sculpture from their kitchen window. Beyond the round forms of box and a holly tree (*Ilex aquifolium*), tall bamboos screen neighbouring houses.

131

ABOVE A closer view of the ceramic bird sculpture by Maria Börjesson, hunched on his twin stakes, by the entrance path. OPPOSITE Standing out among the yellow flowers behind an ivy covered trunk is a *Cotinus coggygria* that Bertil Hansson cuts back severely each spring to encourage dark, almost purplish-black leaves later in the year.

and it awakened his interest. He also later realized that it had a number of notable formal features similar to Hidcote. But, one might ask, is it possible to produce a compartmental garden when the garden's overall surface area is no bigger than a single enclosure of its great models? Bertil would of course reply, 'It's not impossible.' His cleverly sub-divided garden, full of nooks and crannies, certainly gives the impression of being much bigger than more open plan gardens of the same size in the neighbourhood.

From the beginning Bertil built a 'circular tour' into his design through more or less closed rooms and sections, with the occasional vista into other spaces. We experience a rhythm between light, open, larger spaces and dark, enclosed, smaller spaces, similar to walking through a medieval town such as Siena, where narrow shady streets always lead into a light square. The 'piazza' in Bertil's garden is in front of the house –

the central lawn between the hedge walls. It gathers light reflected by the water channel and provides the essential free, restful space within the calculated and very full staged effects.

But now we move on to Bertil Hannson's astounding colour compositions· in borders of perennials and his rich experience within this garden of plants that prefer shade.

By the rounded box shapes an orange-yellow and black ceramic bird sculpture announces a flower bed that is planted mainly with yellow-leaved plants; it is inviting and joyous even on dark, dismal days. The whole area is covered with the small-leaved spindle bush (*Euonymus fortunei* 'Emerald 'n' Gold'), half-hidden under bushes with golden-yellow foliage, such as mock orange (*Philadelphus coronarius* 'Aureus'), red-berried elder (*Sambucus racemosa* 'Plumosa Aurea'), yellow *Berberis* and perhaps the most beautiful of these yellow-leaved plants, *Pleioblastus auricomus*, a small bush bamboo, that grows only half-a-metre (20 inches) tall, if cut back each year. Even an ivy takes on this colour, climbing up the stem of a *Gleditsia* 'Sunburst', that does justice to its name. But enough of yellow.

Bertil now surprises us with a red-leaved smokebush (*Cotinus coggygria*) and further contrasts to the yellow scene, provided by the dark reddish leaves and coral-pink flowers of *Heuchera* 'Palace Purple' and the small, naturally round, compact red shapes of *Berberis thunbergii*. In the spring there are orange tulips and milkweed (*Euphorbia griffithii* 'Dixter'), which has bronze-tinted leaves on into the summer.

A light space divider made of plaited willow, almost covered by plants, marks the boundary to the next garden between the boundary and the yew hedge. For a number of years, taller, silver-grey willow shrubs, such as the woolly willow (*Salix lanata*) and the Swiss willow (*S. helvetica*), dominated this space with the yew backdrop, which was complemented by silver-grey and bluish-grey perennials. A fascinating bed of grey tones gave a strong contrast to the adjoining yellow grouping. But most of the willows contracted a fungal disease and extremely damp autumn and winter weather decimated this grey-leaved collection. The flower bed behind the hedge is now dominated by flowers on the blue-red colour scale, from light pink to dark purple, with some yellow intermingled for contrast. A screen made of black-painted wooden battens shields the garden from the neighbours, giving a dark background to heighten the effect of the flower colours. Today it is almost completely covered by a choice collection of clematis such as 'Victoria', 'Etoile Violette', 'Mme Julia Correvon' and 'Mrs T. Lundell' in colours from dark violet to light lilac. A clever

LEFT Beyond the perfectly clipped yew hedge lies a narrow flower bed arranged around a handsome teak bench with planting in mauves, pinks and silver-grey.

RIGHT The bench and its backing of clematis and honeysuckle remain from year to year, as does the carpet of New Zealand burr (*Acaena buchananii*), but the perennials constantly change. Here the perennial climber everlasting pea (*Lathyrus grandiflorus*) with mallow and cranesbill (*Geranium endressii*), with its brighter pink, form a scene which Bertil remembers with particular pleasure.

FAR RIGHT, ABOVE *Geranium psilostemon* and *Delphinium* 'Black Knight', and BELOW *Knautia macedonica* and *Artemisia ludoviciana* 'Silver Queen'.

complement to these strong vertical colours is provided by a further, rarely seen climber, the honeysuckle *Lonicera prolifera* with its beautiful greyish-blue foliage and with unusually large sepals of the same harmonizing colour.

Since the family is mostly away in high summer, floral effects were planned increasingly for early and late summer. In late spring to early summer Armenian cranesbill (*Geranium psilostemon*) is in flower with its vibrant magenta colour and unusual black centres, toned down by a planting of the 'Black Knight' species of delphinium. From midsummer to September the intensive colour of these cranesbills is repeated, but more modestly in the form of the *Psilostemon* hybrid 'Patricia', which Bertil recommends because it flowers for a long time and nicely retains its low height. In midsummer and autumn the sage *Salvia nemorosa* 'Amethyst' is added to this grouping, which is located close to the strongly tinted cranesbills. In August violet phlox and the irrepressibly multiplying light mauve goat's rue (*Galega officinalis*) flower in this corner.

Bertil likes plants that English gardeners call 'weavers', which are not well-behaved enough to stay where they are planted but get the better of their situation and spread, so making their surroundings appear more natural. That is the case with most species of *Artemisia*, which provide important harmonizing grey tones. Other 'intermediaries' spread easily through seeding, such as the pale pink version of toad flax (*Linaria purpurea* 'Canon J. Went'), which Bertil usually leaves wherever it turns up. Each summer he plants annual violet-blue *Verbena bonariensis*, particularly in the foreground. Their light, panicle-like cymes, up to 1.5 metres (5 feet) tall, do not obstruct the view through the flower bed; in this way it gains in depth. He uses *Verbena hastata* 'Rosea' in the same way as a contrast, for in Lund this overwinters as a perennial, whereas *V. bonariensis* is not winter hardy. By the seat with its underplanting of New Zealand burr (*Acaena buchananii*) ,patches of sage (*Salvia argentea*) have to be replaced after a wet winter, and blue oat grass (*Helictotrichon sempervirens*) provide tall and powerful accentuation above the living carpet. A constant background to the perennials and light grey bench is a *Rosa rubrifolia* (syn. *Rosa glauca*) which, like the honeysuckle *Lonicera prolifera* with its vertical foliage, provides a background of changing colour. It mediates between the colours of the perennials and the grasses. In Hillier's

Manual of Trees and Shrubs this remarkable plant is described as follows: 'The great attraction of this rose is its foliage, which is glaucous-purple in a sunny position and a greyish green, with a mauve tinge when in shade.'

A group of late-summer flowering plants has been added in recent years. They include loosestrife (*Lythrum salicaria* 'Blush') with its long-flowering, beautiful pink racemes, close to the bistort *Persicaria amplexicaulis* 'Rosea', that hails from the Himalayas. Between them is the genuine Swedish variety 'Magnus' of the coneflower *Echinacea purpurea*, overshadowed by the purplish-black flowerheads of the tall perennial Joe Pye weed, *Eupatorium purpureum* 'Atropurpureum'. This is a clone of *E.p.* subsp. *maculatum*, whose big purple-pinkish flat-topped panicles are repeated later on in the shorter orpine (*Sedum telephium*). The star-shaped flowers of masterwort (*Astrantia major*), and its wine-red variety 'Hadspen' and lighter variety 'Lars', complete this late summer scene.

A Japanese-inspired decorative space-divider separates this main flower bed from the 'Japanese area', that lies in half-shade. Here, in this extremely constricted place, using bamboos, Bertil has set up a small fountain and a 'hovering' seat hung between two very effective, round red posts. Beautiful polished stones from the river, gravel and a bonsai-like dwarf elm round off this scene. Over a few flat stepping stones, smoothed by a hot finish with a welding torch, the short but eventful path continues through a narrow, dark passage. With the light conditions of an Italian grotto, it brings memories of Dante's *Inferno*, but then comes the vista of a small *Paradiso* – the open view of a green oasis where a water channel, shining invitingly in the sun, ripples along the lawn. A miniature alpine garden in stone troughs, Bertil's most recent creation, is at the far end.

A few steps across the sunny lawn takes us to the shade garden, which lies between two tall hornbeam hedges. Here beneath two American mountain ash trees (*Sorbus americana*) and a few smaller Japanese maples, Bertil has created an attractively intimate atmosphere, a jungle with bamboos, ferns and the large, massed foliage of *Rodgersia*. A few Japanese painted ferns (*Athyrium niponicum* var. *pictum*) have slowly spread to form a silver-grey mat flushed with maroon, a beautiful contrast with blue-leaved plantain lilies (*Hosta sieboldiana* var. *elegans*). One Japanese maple is bedded on a carpet of asarabacca (*Asarum europaeum*) which stretches up

135

OPPOSITE Looking back down the lawn towards the house, sunlight shines on the brick-edged water rill running parallel with the yew hedge. It was added in the late 1980s. This small channel, just a half-metre (20 inches) wide and barely a metre (3 feet) in depth, lies between a stone trough alpine garden by the seat and a small pond in the Japanese garden.

ABOVE A few former feeding troughs from Austria with tiny mountain plants and precious succulents and round stones form a framework that fits in economically between the yew hedge and the start of the lawn. Such an attractive little trough garden saves the mostly pointless effort of trying to reproduce natural-looking, mountainous terrain on flat ground.

BELOW The Japanese-inspired space divider consists of black-painted vertical battens, 10 centimetres (4 inches) in width, with two to four sticks of bamboo between each batten. The dwarf elm *Ulmus* 'Jacqueline Hillier' and a small salix on the left frame a 'Tsukubai' water spout.

ABOVE The shade garden lies between hornbeam hedges. In the foreground to the left is a *Kirengeshoma palmata* with the big leaves of *Astilboides tabularis* behind, while to the right is *Hosta* 'Hydon Sunset'. Between two groups of *Hosta* 'Buchshaw Blue' is black 'grass', otherwise lilyturf blackdragon (*Ophiopogon planiscapus* 'Nigrescens'), a lily from Japan that needs protection in winter.

to the windbreak of the protective hedge where the giant leaves of *Astilboides tabularis* stand out, echoing in some way the shape of the much smaller wild ginger. In spring, a multitude of pale blue wood anemones (*Anemone nemorosa*) flower together with bloodroot (*Sanguinaria canadensis* f. *multiplex*) with its white cup-shaped flowers, followed by long-flowering *Geranium macrorrhizum* with its panicles of white to purplish-red flowers and shining red leaves in the autumn.

The brown-brick square atrium garden, some 60 metres (70 yards) square, is surrounded by the two-storey house, with its single-storey wings and a wooden garage and small workshop on the fourth side. In the morning it lies in shadow. A small fountain plays in a brown ceramic container and around the beautiful slate table are four elegant chairs created by the Swedish architect Josef Frank (his family came from Austria). His gracious, relaxed designs – now experiencing a revival – strongly influenced the style that in the New York World Exhibition of 1939 became known as 'Swedish Modern'.

This interior courtyard is full of atmosphere. The flower beds in front of the buildings are of differing widths and raised up a little within brick edgings, so that the terrace takes on an attractive, slightly sunken look.

Viewed from inside the house, this beautiful interior courtyard gains in depth. The branches of the exotic shrubs *Cornus kousa* var. *chinensis* and *Sorbus koehneana* are a foil to the numerous stems of the snake-bark maple (*Acer capillipes*) from Japan. Where there is more sunshine, blue 'wish' flowers dominate – 'wish' because contrary to descriptions in perennial catalogues they often take on a lilac colour, especially in photographs. Bertil always combines the blue with some yellow or orange and is wont to quote Van Gogh: 'If you are painting blue, then yellow and orange as well.' He gets the bluish-lilac colour mostly from different kinds of cranebills such as the wood cranesbill (*Geranium sylvaticum* 'Mayflower'), from mid-May onwards, followed by the variety 'Johnson's Blue' and the more recent, similar kind 'Brookside', that has a second crop of flowers in the autumn. In late summer he has perhaps the most beautiful of all the geraniums, the really clear-blue 'Buxton's Variety', a variety of *G. wallichianum* from Nepal. Noticeable among the yellow contrast flowers is a long-spurred columbine, its gracious flowers hovering like butterflies over the dark blue of the sage *Salvia* 'Mainacht'. Here and there the leaves and yellowish green, loose yet ample flowers of lady's mantle (*Alchemilla mollis*) hang over the edges of the bricks. A few day lilies contribute some yellow and

in a rather shady corner the yellow and orange flowers of the Welsh poppy (*Meconopsis cambrica*) form the vibrant background for the violet-blue flowers of the wood cranesbill. To get more variation in the blue-yellow grouping, the clinging magenta-coloured cranesbill (*Geranium* 'Ann Folklard') is permitted to entwine its upright partners among the others, as well as the sage and bellflowers (*Campanula* spp.).

Over the years Bertil Hansson has developed and refined his gardening talents as a means of relaxation. He and his wife Eva are both senior lecturers at the ancient University of Lund, she in chemistry and he in electronics. Strolling through this small garden we have experienced clearly structured spaces filled with colour and scent and illusions, which enchant the visitor and probably also lend a little magic to the life of Bertil and Eva Hansson themselves.

OPPOSITE Late evening in the atrium garden, where two *Cornus kousa* var. *chinensis* frame drifts of acid-green *Alchemilla mollis* flowers and a brown ceramic trough with a fountain.

BELOW The shadiest corner is occupied by an admirable, small collection of plantain lilies with their blue-and-green colours that contrast with yellows, such as a yellowish-green striped grass answering to the tongue twisting name of *Hakonechloa macra* 'Aureola'. *Lysimachia nummularia* 'Aurea' encroaches over attractive round ceramic slabs.

ABOVE The richly warm red garden gate leads onto the street.
BELOW a shining blue cloth-sculpture and pennant signal a
welcome. OPPOSITE By the garden door the delicate pink
blooms of *Rosa* 'New Dawn' spread in a sea of lavender.

Courtyard Garden in Green & Blue

The Nordström family's blue house lies in the picturesque old quarter of Simrishamn, a little town on the south-east coast of Skåne with fishing harbours where sailors like to anchor and boats leave for the nearby island of Bornholm. On opening the oxblood-red gate you don't at once see the garden, but find yourself in a narrow passage opposite two plane trees. A strip of blue cloth curtain hung on a stand with two iron legs catches the eye, and two pebble islands around the trunks of two plane trees enliven the concrete paving stones. After the spartan entrance, behind the house you are met by an astonishing oasis of scent and bloom. It is a mere 115 metres (138 yards) square, but by clever subdivision landscape architect Tommy Nordström has gained an astounding amount of space for his family.

Four diagonal box hedges frame two beds, each surrounded by square concrete paving slabs. The main path is the width of two slabs, which at 80 centimetres (32 inches) still allows for a comfortable stroll through the lush green of the garden. The house connects directly with the garden by Nordström's clever design, which extends the lines of the box hedges, broken by the path, right up to its blue walls. Three pine trellises entwined with *Wisteria sinensis* create a further division along the wall of the house. Beneath the windows, which are painted a very dark green with a white surround, an area the width of four paving slabs has been transformed into a series of little rooms and niches. With their trellises and low-growing evergreen hedges planted at right angles to the house, the rooms create both variety and a sense of security, while also having the effect of extending the small garden. By accommodating unexpected views, at no point can the little landscape be surveyed in one glance, which might become boring.

Trellises and fences planted with climbers are a space-saving way of providing vertical greenery and can usefully take the place of a medium shrub or even a small tree. In Nordström's garden the fences are smothered in ivy, the evergreen *Lonicera henryi* and the colourful foliage of *Actinidia kolomikta*. But to do without trees entirely, the garden would lack atmosphere.

Simrishamn, Sweden

ABOVE When the wisteria's beautiful blooms appear (at the end of May in southern Sweden and Denmark), against the walls they make a stunning rhapsody in lilac and blue. In summer we must be content with the spikes of peach-leaved bellflower (*Campanula persicifolia*). BELOW In the foreground feathered leaves of *Ailanthus altissima* frame grassy *Tradescantia* x *andersoniana*, rounded box forms and drifts of lavender.

ABOVE A fig tree thriving at the window in Tommy Nordström's garden is a surprising sight though admittedly it is more of a shrub than a tree. In front a standard gooseberry, the pale pink of the rose 'New Dawn' and a silver-grey sage (*Salvia officinalis*). BELOW A circular island of pebbles around the trunk of a plane tree enlivens the ribbed concrete paving stones of the passageway.

Nordström has planted his trees at the edge of the garden to leave the view clear in the middle. Which varieties of tree are 'suitable' for a town garden of this sort? Nordström has chosen an *Ailanthus altissima*, which has fronds up to 70 centimetres (27 inches) long, to give a distinctly tropical effect. (Though it grows tall, it can be cut right back each year until it takes on the form of a huge, untamed fern rather than a tree.) A walnut tree has been planted in the corner of the terrace next to the house and another at the entrance to the passage. And then a real surprise in this northerly garden: a mulberry tree growing against the brown toolshed. Admittedly it is the hardier variety *Morus nigra* (not the *M. alba* beloved of silk worms). It grows slowly and even though still small takes on a characteristically gnarled shape. Remarkably, the fig tree (*Ficus carica*) is a member of the mulberry family, although its deeply-lobed leaves bear no resemblance to its relative. Here in southern Sweden it is no more than a shrub, supported on a trellis.

The two box-edged beds are planted in blue and white to echo the colour of the house. A few balls of box and mounds of lavender give structure to the larger bed. In early spring there are scented narcissi (*Narcissus poeticus*) in the purest of whites and *Pulmonaria* 'Mrs Moon', its leaves sprinkled with silver; in March *Omphalodes verna*, their little blossoms like forget-me-nots, create a shimmer of sky blue. The smaller bed near the seating area is at its peak in June when the white peony

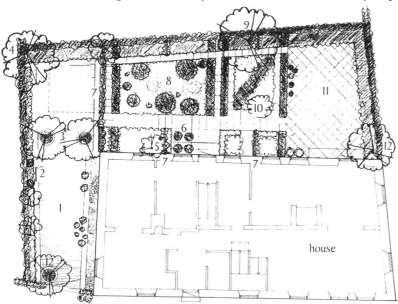

1 passage to garden	5 fig tree	9 *Ailanthus altissima*
2 cloth-sculpture	6 pots with herbs	10 bamboo (now dead)
3 plane trees	7 wisteria on fence	11 sitting area
4 mulberry tree	8 spheres of box	12 walnut trees

ABOVE The fresh young leaves of *Wisteria sinensis* are a gleaming yellowy-green with just a flush of red. They make a lovely contrast to the deeper foliage of the climbers that form the backdrop to Tommy Nordström's garden. BELOW Mauve-pink marguerites (*Erigeron* 'Foerster's Liebling', bred by Karl Foerster of Potsdam) jostle against box with the grass-like leaves and blue flowers of *Tradescantia* x *andersoniana*.

143

ABOVE The blue cloth floats on the breeze next to two mophead plane trees in front of a brown tool shed. Along the blue-painted wall, white pebbles and a white-painted vertical edge at the corner add freshness in this largely shady corner.

OPPOSITE There is a jaunty, southern feel to the small garden behind the blue house in Simrishamn, with its blue and purple flowers and air of relaxation. Here you can see clearly how the low box hedges and balls give shape to the beds, dividing them into smaller 'rooms'.

(*Paeonia lactiflora*) comes into bloom next to the violet flowers and reed-like leaves of *Iris sibirica*. In August the blue umbels of the fully hardy *Agapanthus campanulatus* dominate. Asters provide an autumn finale: *A. amellus* 'King George' in deep violet-blue and *A. dumosus* 'Schneekissen', whose pure white flowers bloom into October. Finally, the lovely autumn colours of the evergreen shrub *Viburnum* x *burkwoodii* with its gleaming droplets of red among glossy dark green foliage form a hedge by the terrace and complete the picture.

Nowhere in this garden can one lose sight of the blue of the house; it is a constant presence that not everyone could live with, but it changes throughout the day according to the light. Tommy Nordström mixed the ultramarine from an old recipe for oil and egg tempera: one part linseed oil to one part raw egg, two parts water and a small amount of pigment (ultramarine and a little zinc white). This works out considerably cheaper than a commercially-mixed paint, but when the façade is repainted every eight years another 330 eggs must be sacrificed.

Geometry in Yellow & Green

The task of designing his or her own garden gives a landscape architect the rare chance to fulfil long-cherished wishes. Andreas Bruun was attracted by the possibility of playing with classic geometric forms such as spheres, triangles and parabolas, curves which especially fascinate astronomers, who watch the paths of comets. Bruun chose arcs from the universe like comet trajectories to give dynamic form to his designs for grass lawns. The story of this geometrical transformation of lawns started just ten years ago when the Bruun family bought their classic 1929 house with its warm yellow walls.

The thousand-square-metre (quarter-acre) area behind the house had the usual over-sized and boring rectangular lawn, which left only narrow strips at the sides for flowering shrubs

and bushes. Another problem was the raised, unprotected and badly proportioned terrace alongside the house which was hemmed in by a flower bed and too cramped for enjoying time outside. A narrow slope leading up from the lower lawn gave added emphasis to the stiff concrete steps in its middle.

In the total revamping of the garden the terrace was enlarged to form a rectangle 10.5 by 3 metres (33 by 10 feet). In place of an unattractive slope, a difference in height of about one metre (3 feet) was overcome partly by means of walls constructed of simple grey concrete blocks, which could hold smaller plants, and partly by a bold remodelling of the earth. Two small curved hills, covered with soft planting, enfold the steps, partially masking them. Where they meet the lawn, these charming twin

Køge, Denmark

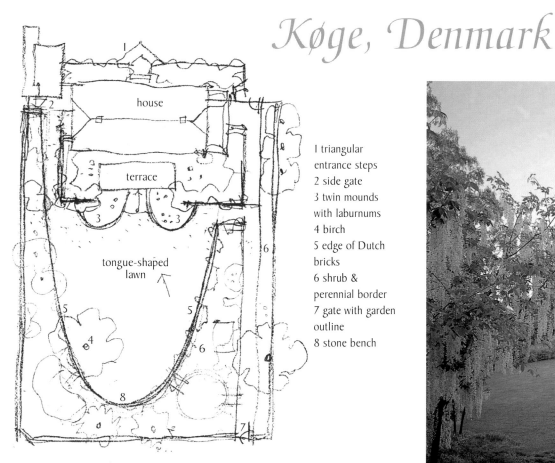

1 triangular entrance steps
2 side gate
3 twin mounds with laburnums
4 birch
5 edge of Dutch bricks
6 shrub & perennial border
7 gate with garden outline
8 stone bench

LEFT Foreground poppies (*Papaver nudicaule*) pick up the bright yellow of the laburnums that screen the warm yellow house. The parabola of bricks enclosing the lawn is repeated in brick surrounds to the twin mounds below the terrace.
RIGHT Pink rhododendrons and a slender conifer are the focus across the spacious arc of lawn, its dynamic shape firmly anchored by a stately birch.

mounds are edged with a ribbon border of yellow Dutch bricks.

The change from a rectangular to curved lawn, contained within a parabola arc of the same yellow bricks, was carried out according to the laws of geometry. The symmetrical axis runs at right angles to the entrance to the house. However, for optical and for practical reasons Bruun rounded off the mathematical curve a little at the lawn's southern end where the two brick sides of the parabola meet. A few metres farther south there is a small stone bench on the symmetrical axis where the flower bed starts. From this bench one can enjoy the best view of the fine house and the dynamic motion of the brick arcs.

After the house and garden had come together, Andreas Bruun married the colours. He matched the warm yellow of the house walls with a dozen laburnums for dramatic yellow in spring, four each on the twin hillocks and two each to the right and left, by the corners of the house under the gable ends. The trees, which are pruned annually, give the effect from the terrace of a flowering screen. The shining yellow is followed a few weeks later by the contrasting blue of three Chinese wisterias (*Wisteria sinensis*), which climb the house on white trellises. On the centre mounds under the laburnums spread scented thyme and juniper (*Juniperus pfitzeriana* 'Wilhelm Pfitzer').

In the flower beds around the lawn *Rhododendron* 'Catawbiense grandiflorum', *Amelanchier laevis* and *Tsuga canadensis*, seven of each species or variety, are distributed to form a flowering and evergreen rhythm. A few big concrete spheres shine white among the foxgloves and the spheroid shape is repeated in miniature on the western garden gate. But the game of playing with forms starts in front of the house, where the steps leading up to the entrance form a pyramid. Exactly above, a gable window repeats the triangle.

Bruun employed the triangle in his design for the square in front of the main entrance to the Royal Agricultural and Veterinary University in Copenhagen. In the middle of a box-lined parterre he set a wonderful pyramid-shaped fountain. He has also received the honour of election to the committee in charge of Karen Blixen's Rungstedlund Foundation.

A touch of magic awaits visitors entering the garden from the south side. If they are unfamiliar with the garden, they can see in the ironwork of the garden gate a long-nosed face, a strange face that appears to smile. Seconds later the nose turns out to be a parabola, the eyes two hillocks and the crown on its head the house itself, with its triangular steps at the top. The whole ground plan is present in the hammered ironwork of the gate, a surprise announcement of things to come.

LEFT The white front door leads directly onto the pavement without a fence. Running the length of the façade is a raised bed with evergreen box, *Taxus* and *Viburnum rhytidophyllum* and underneath the green groundcover of *Waldsteinia ternata*. Climbing the white trellis are *Clematis alpina* and *macropetala* (since replaced with evergreen *Lonicera henryi*, which keeps its leaves in winter and accentuates the peace here in front of the house). The raised bed is contained by a wall, built of concrete, which merges with the triangular steps of the same construction and height. A litle group of birches and robinias throw light shade on to anyone who passes.

LEFT The triangular stairs open out after the fourth step onto a clinker-brick terrace where vistors are greeted by a droll stone elephant. On stepping out of the house one can set off to either right or left, to the beach or the town. The little terrace provides a place to pause and collect one's thoughts, or to have a last chat with the family.

RIGHT At the far end of the garden an ironwork gate has a gnomish expression, but it turns out to have a different and more symbolic significance.

Wildwood, Flowers & Mountain Plants

Midsummer in Sweden. When the sun reaches its zenith, there are celebrations and dancing and the girls weave floral wreaths in their hair. Here, near a light-coloured house, the Himalayan birch tree was lithe and slender, with bright daisies encircling its snow-white trunk. I came across this lovely tree at the start of a walk through Eva and Roland Gustavsson's garden, not far from the old university town of Lund. Here in Dalby, on the edge of the range of hills of Romelåsen, with a view of the fields and woods in the blue distance, these two landscape architects, both lecturers at the University of Agricultural Sciences at Alnarp, have used their expertise to make two terraces out of a south-facing slope, some 650 square metres (780 square yards) in size, in a fairly densely developed estate.

The two levels are planted in quite different ways. In the upper part, where the Himalayan birch tree (*Betula utilis* var. *jacquemontii* 'Doorenbos') stands, are silver-grey creeping plants, such as cat's ears (*Antennaria*) and grey-leaved thyme, and stones to hint at a mountain landscape. Here too are other trees with ornamental barks: the Manchurian cherry (*Prunus maackii*), a rare tree from Korea and Manchuria with a shiny, yellow-brownish bark but fully hardy in winter temperatures; and *Prunus avium*, the native wild cherry with shining brown bark and small, sweet fruit and white cherry blossom, which is also fully hardy and more frost-resistant than the Japanese cherry. In spring, beneath these trees with different-coloured barks, is a spread of wild flowers such as the yellow wood anemone (*A. ranunculoides*), white windflower (*A. nemorosa*), and *Corydalis cava* with its purple flowers. These are followed from May to September on the sunnier side of the path by perennials such as cowslips (*Primula veris*), the peach-leaved bellflower (*Campanula persicifolia*) and bloody cranesbill (*Geranium sanguineum*), with its shining crimson flowers.

Still on the upper level of the garden, close to the house and sheltered by a hornbeam hedge, there is a beautiful terrace of dark brown sandstone containing a water garden which runs diagonally across the terrace and which can be seen from the house windows. The same stone is used for steps and walls in the lower garden and comes from a nearby quarry; its colour harmonizes with the plants and the water. Soft rain water from the roof collects in this small water garden. Rushes such as *Schoenoplectus lacustris* subsp. *tabernaemontani* 'Zebrinus' and dwarf bulrushes (*Typha minima*) grow in the water, whereas palm branch sedge (*Carex muskingumensis*) and *Spodiopogon sibiricus* flourish in the damp bog-like area.

Irises have been added to the filigree of grasses. Those species that prefer damp conditions, such as the Siberian iris (*Iris sibirica*), the yellow flag iris (*I. pseudacorus*) and the blue flag iris (*I. versicolor*) are played off against those species that prefer dry conditions, such as the bearded irises, *I.* 'Maori King' with its yellowish-brown and purple and *I.* 'Joanna Taylor' with its bluish-purple colouring. This surprising effect is possible because water, damp places and sun-warmed stone are all so close together. Thyme (*Thymus serpyllum*) and *Leptinella minor* (syn. *Cotula minor*) creep between cracks in the natural stone. Small botanic tulips flower in the spring followed by the prairie quamash (*Camassia leichtlinii* subsp. *leichtlinii*) with its creamy-white flowers later on. In late summer flower colour is concentrated on the façade of the house where the rose 'New Dawn' and *Clematis* 'Mrs T. Lundell' intertwine.

Continuing down steps made from the dark brown natural stone we come to the lower level with its more luxuriant vegetation of broad-leafed trees and bushes rich in blossoms. Here there are magnolias, the snowdrop tree (*Halesia carolina*), the green- and-white-striped snake-bark maple (*Acer rufinerve*) from the mountain slopes of Japan, as well as a multitude of rhododendrons, followed by hydrangeas that blossom later in the summer. It is a densely planted 'woodland' area, a small jungle with clearings, where the plants are not pampered as individual rare pieces of a collection, but deliberately exposed to hard competition. This makes it possible to study the living conditions of a plant community and observe which plants come out on top in the competition for light. In drier summers competition for water is noticeable – the rhododendrons hold their own, but the hydrangeas soon flop.

This dense planting, which at the outset achieved quick results, does require that plants must now and again be cut back. The Gustavssons make good use of their garden shears not only to direct the interplay of the trees and bushes but also

Dalby, Sweden

ABOVE The front of the house, looking towards the entrance to the garden. The grass path is bordered by white flowers of *Saxifraga cuneifolia* and *Vancouveria hexandra* behind, with *Euonymus planipes* and *Actinidia kolomikta* above and *Salix koriyanagi* on the left.

RIGHT The white Himalayan birch (*Betula utilis* var. *jacquemontii* 'Doorenbos') decked with daisies in a dazzling display of white against the deep shade of the border along the grass path.

FOLLOWING PAGES, LEFT Grass paths weave along the lower garden past the open vertical screen of bare *Amelanchier spicata* stems and shrub and perennial borders to the small woodland and peat garden, originally created for the Gustavsson's son, Mattis. RIGHT Looking the other way, with the amelanchier stems on the left, through to the neighbours' garden – the hedge was removed by friendly agreement some years ago. In the foreground is *Hemerocallis* 'Golden Chimes' with *Osmunda regalis*.

to encourage special shapes. The lower shoots of the juneberry (*Amelanchier spicata*), a shrub originally from the forests and rocky areas of north-eastern America and now widespread in the open countryside of Sweden, are removed so that the individual dark brown stems stand out. They rise straight up, marking the confines of a space, yet also granting a vista into the next green chamber. If the owners find this reliable bush getting too big, they can always cut it right back so that the next growth of 'spears' may perhaps shoot up even straighter. The cleanly formed stems give protection to various perennials, such as lady's mantle (*Alchemilla mollis*), *Geranium endressii* and wild ginger (*Asarum europaeum*) with its winter-green, shining kidney-shaped leaves. These low perennials growing between the stems of the shrub are highly visible because they are not covered by its twigs, and so the scene gains in clarity.

In contrast to the flowing areas between the trees and open shrubs, which give unexpected and delightful perspectives, tall hornbeam hedges pointedly mark off the last of the spaces. They mask neighbouring houses without completely obscuring the beautiful background landscape when the garden is viewed from the upper level. The hedges form green sculptures that curve up the slope and lend a dynamic quality to this part of the garden, near the pond. One of them becomes ever narrower the higher it rises up the slope; at the top it becomes almost horizontal, like a hovering long neck of some fabled or prehistoric creature. Sunlight floods through a round window in one hedge lower down and we look expectantly into the furthest garden chamber which houses a forest of woodland miniatures.

In this small, quiet moss-covered garden with its low pine hedge and bizarre dwarf birch trees, you might think you are in the land of Lilliput. Gradually adapting to the dimensions, I squat down on the ground, frog-like, with my camera: bilberry and cranberry bushes become small trees, just like in Elsa Beskov's picture book, *Putte in the Bilberry Wood*. This garden used to belong to the Gustavssons' now-adult son Mattis, who as a small boy wished to transport his grandfather's wood to this spot and have his own place to sit. So his parents made him a small wild garden, a biotope, with mostly native plants from the woodland and high-lying moors, and dwarf trees and bushes from the mountains. The small slope was terraced with stones and blocks of peat. Sackloads of pine needles, brought from the woods, created the right mix of loose peat and pine needles needed as the basis for a community of acid soil-loving plants. Miniature bogs were created by laying out plastic pond sheeting and covering it with layers of shining white sphagnum moss that soaks up water like a sponge.

When everything had been properly prepared, the planting could begin. The astounding thing here was that plants taken from the wild and plants bought at garden centres and nurseries all felt equally at home. Right from the beginning this little garden gave the impression of being perfectly finished and complete and since then has required little work. The only problem is that birds take the peat moss to build their nests.

Around where Mattis used to have his seat there is a group of multi-stemmed dwarf Erman's birches (*Betula ermanii* 'Mount Apoi') and small mountain willows (*Salix hastata*) which emphasize the mountain character of the spot. A common Scots pine (*Pinus sylvestris*) regularly has its crown lopped off. Heather flowers in this small wilderness and there are plants from the high-lying moors: marsh ledum (*Ledum palustre*), a one-metre (3-foot) high shrub with narrow, leathery leaves and an aromatic scent; *Empetrum nigrum*, a small shrub with black berries; and sweet gale (*Myrica gale*). But this is the land of Carl von Linné; the delicate little beauty named after him is also a must, the twin-flower (*Linnaea borealis*), a dwarf shrub that flowers from June to August with little pink or white bells striped red on the inside. Keeping this Swedish plant company are three North American plants, *Rhododendron vaseyi*, with gleaming white flowers of wood lilies (*Trillium*) close by, and *Rhododendron canadense*. In places we are surprised by the bright violet flowers of the spotted orchid (*Dactylorhiza maculata*), the dainty blossoms of cyclamens (*Cyclamen hederifolium*) and, later in the autumn, by deep blue gentians (*Gentiana sino-ornata*). This small community from the peat moorlands of course hates calcium-rich tap water.

If you walk through this sloping garden of many contrasts at different times of day, you can experience the changing effects of light and shadow. It is a theatre of flowers, where some scenes are effective in the morning sun and others develop their colours and shapes later in the day. This play of light was consciously built into the garden by its 'stage managers'. In the evening, when the trees and bushes at the lower pond cast their long shadows on the turf path, the surface of the water begins to shine, and the royal ferns (*Osmunda regalis*) and the warm yellow of the daylilies (*Hemerocallis*) become transparent against the light, the garden gains a further dimension. The boundary to the neighbour's garden was removed by mutual agreement years ago and the gardens have grown together. Two gardens without limit: is that not a happy ending to the story?

Exotic Courtyard with Pink & Gold

When you see this small garden courtyard for the first time, you might think you are somewhere in the Far East. The elderly lady with the youthful smile, dressed entirely in violet up to her wide headband, is used to visitors being rendered speechless at the sight of her garden.

Tucked between the house and an outhouse set at right angles to it, and two high, screening black wooden walls, this small garden, under 100 square metres (120 square yards) in size, is filled with sculptures and decorative objects made of pottery, iron, plaster, glass and wood, and a magnificent display of flowers. Yet despite all this abundance everything is governed by a sense of shape and order, in which symmetry and recurrent colours play a role. At the start of September, for example, there will be a repetition of the white of the hydrangeas (*Hydrangea arborescens* 'Annabelle'), the red of fuchsias and the pale pink of small roses and the strong blue and pink of the painted furniture and the decor. Four square white wooden posts, the top ends of which are decorated and each of which carries a small ceramic sculpture – a blue bull, a white cat and two old faded birds from Bornholm – on a wooden platform that is painted pink are the most important vertical features in this small garden. They mark off the area of the spectacular flower bed in the middle where a small square stone bath has been erected as a fountain. It is a raised stone island with coloured glass balls and a stylized iron plant with a gigantic flower, painted pink, of course. In this central flowerbed, where small white marguerites and red sweet peas flower and squares of box form the transition to the paved path, there is a small forest of black poles, each one with two dangerously glinting gilded halberds and spears, as well as black iron lanterns draped with

Brantevik, Sweden

drops of crystal that reflect the sunlight, producing wonderful refractions. At each corner of this magical flower bed, blue-painted, gracefully formed Norwegian lamps from the turn of the last century look like giant blue bell flowers. Here an Oregon grape (*Mahonia aquifolium*) colludes with an old black-iron churchyard cross with gold decoration; growing out of the top of the evergreen shrub is a blue-green ceramic head from the East with a crown of 'gold' on its head.

You have to walk step by step along the paved paths to examine this small kingdom with its multitude of remarkable details; surrounding the planting the paths become areas of pebble. Then other objects turn up, like so many pieces of evidence: left and right of the main bed, with its profusion of vertical lines, colours and sparkling light, there are groups of large box spheres. The green shapes are reminiscent of old, round-bellied terracotta receptacles, and each has a 'lid' topped by a golden orb.

Karin Wassberg, the lady in violet, has gilded the light wood

halls and other decorative objects in her garden, for gold work, together with arts-and-crafts work, is her main profession. She has commissions in museums and even in a royal Swedish palace. Two Greek coryphaei, which she 'magicked' here from a museum (not the originals, of course, but plaster copies) are painted so that they have a hint of patina; they flank the small summer house with its decorated white gable. Next to the right-hand coryphaeus and a summerhouse wall painted with purple-black and white squares, there is a blue form that looks reminiscent of a gothic church window frame – and it really is such a thing! A pink-coloured stick divides the empty space of the pointed frame into two halves and continues on a little to carry a small ceramic bird on a round plate. Red fuchsias hang around this remarkable composition, which is repeated several times in different variations, sometimes with small-flowered pink roses, sometimes without.

One is amazed how the magician produces combinations in the decoration, changing simple things into bizarre finds. Two

OPPOSITE LEFT & RIGHT Karin Wassberg's courtyard is a treasure trove of strange creatures and simple objects, placed with meticulous care to entrance and delight the visitor.

BELOW LEFT & RIGHT The 'found objects' include statuary and these heads, one embellished with a gilded water-lily crown and collar, the other wreathed in clematis seedheads.

ABOVE A large golden-orange pumpkin, left as if by way of an offering to the gilded statue of a saint on a high plinth. The striking blue is echoed around the garden, here in a gothic frame and chair against red-flowered fuchsias.

RIGHT The refreshing white of *Hydrangea paniculata* contrasts with red roses, blue campanulas and the livid blue and pink of the railing.

OPPOSITE Three of the four white poles, placed in a square, give the strongest vertical accent in the garden, with golden halberds. The upturned spikes of a monkey puzzle tree (*Araucaria araucana*) reinforce the jaunty mood of the garden and guard the box urns, or possibly monks with their gilded tonsures.

cold-blue glass heads from a shop window in Denmark were given warm 'golden' crowns that look like the blossoms of water lilies. Each of these smooth, light-reflecting blue heads rests on something that might be a strange, twisted, pink iron hat-stand around which elegantly gilded flowers climb.

This abundance of elements of such differing styles, from the north and from distant lands, and from such differing epochs, reminds me of Copenhagen's Tivoli with its beautiful atmosphere in the evenings. (The Tivoli dates from the age of eclecticism, which dominated architecture in the nineteenth century, and which espoused the conscious adoption and union of different elements of style which were widely separated in space and time.)

Karin Wassberg calls her small imaginative courtyard garden in Brantevik the 'cloister', for early in the year Madonna lilies blossom in their pure white and, seen at a distance, the plump shapes of box turn into well-nourished monks with golden tonsures who, having endured a fright among the powerful verticals of golden glinting halberds and spears, are turning on their heels as if to flee from the strange creatures.

ABOVE The three roofs of the studio-house rest on huge supporting vertical trunks, and are framed by a hedge of green willow, the purple osier (*Salix purpurea* 'Nana').
OPPOSITE ABOVE A line of silver birches echoes the upright supporting timbers along one side of the office building.
BELOW A side entrance from the courtyard garden leads into the passageway connecting the office building to the studio.

Pekka Salminen's Studio & Garden

Finnish architecture is known everywhere for its simplicity, clarity and respect for nature, and most famously in the work of Alvar Aalto, the shining star of the north. Second only to his buildings are the outside spaces created in relation to them: they are full of poetry. From this heritage surprising forms have been developed in the last few years, using varied materials. A good example of this 'new architecture' is Pekka Salminen's studio-house of 1989, next to his office building constructed fifteen years earlier.

The studio's plunging lines and slanting wooden walls are so full of dramatic tension that they seem almost to have reached the outer limits of equilibrium. From the north-western end of the site, the lightly curved tripartite roof, ranging in height from 7 down to 5 metres (23 to 16 feet), and its black supporting beams suggest the shape of three fans, following each upon the other in diminishing size. The first impression given by this astonishing light brown wooden building, where even the windows have slanting lines, is of a sinking ship – a 'Titantic' atmosphere. This is reinforced by the interior, where in the sophisticated and playful interaction between rectangular, sloping and curved lines, the rules of statics seem to be exploited to the full by the finely balanced supporting forces. The experience is of a completely new space, full of dynamism.

From the largest ground-floor space with its long work table, its sitting area in front of an old tiled fireplace and a hanging model of a boat, a black iron spiral staircase leads up to a balustrade and a suspended upper floor with sauna, bathroom and an area for sleeping. This has a 'rolling' screen, designed by Alvar Aalto, made of narrow, flexible wooden slats. The studio was mainly finished in warm wood and the upper storey in reinforced concrete and grey prefabricated elements of the same material. The architect Pekka Salminen can receive clients and guests here and hold meetings, but also withdraw and relax. (Works by this architectural practice include the municipal theatre of Lahti, the restoration of the Finnish Academy of Music in Helsinki and large projects planned within Helsinki

Helsinki, Finland

Airport at Vantaa terminals, car parks and control tower.)

A short corridor with wooden blinds, through which the sun floods on this August day, links the studio-house and the architect's office proper, a black single-storey wooden building. Unfortunately Pekka Salminen was away on the day of my visit and his place was taken by his friendly son Jarkko, who guided me through the two very different buildings and small garden.

The black façade of the architect's office is visible from the street. Its low windows and protruding roof form a fine contrast to a row of bright birches, which remind us that we are in Finland. These are the common silver birches (*Betula pendula*) with white trunks and graceful, hanging branches; the tree is known as the 'Lady of the Woods'. On its north-western side there is a black-painted pergola-like structure, roofed to give shelter from the rain, used for car parking space. A side entrance into the building is through the same passageway that links it to the spectacular light-brown studio.

In shaping the small garden that lies between the two buildings, Pekka Salminen's aims were to mediate between the two styles of architecture and provide clearly marked pathways to the main and side entrances. Thought also had to be given to the sudden amounts of rainwater that pour down in three places from the studio's tripartite roof. A slightly curved paved path leads to the studio's main entrance; flat, irregular stepping stones in a gently curving area of gravel lead off to the side entrance. A paved rainwater rill takes up superfluous water overflowing from three drainage sumps concealed by gravel and meanders down to a drainage pit at the end of the garden. Strips with larger pebbles along the studio's façade prevent the grey concrete socle of the house and the long, slanting window that almost stretches down to the ground from becoming dirtied with splashes of earth from the rain, which could detract from one's delight in the beautiful little garden.

This small but fine garden that harmoniously links the two so-different houses was designed by landscape architect Gretel Hemgård. Among her projects was the important commission to restore the gardens of Hvitträsk, 30 kilometres (18 miles) to the west of Helsinki. The houses and gardens here, built and developed at the start of the twentieth century, belonged to the influential architects Eliel Saarinen, Hermann Gesellius and Armas Lindgren. Today Hvitträsk, a jewel of Finnish architecture from the age of national romanticism, is a popular museum. She also restored the nineteenth-century Brunnsparken, some forty-odd acres in size, to its former dignity, and planned a new park, Arabianranta – some 120 acres on the city's eastern shore line.

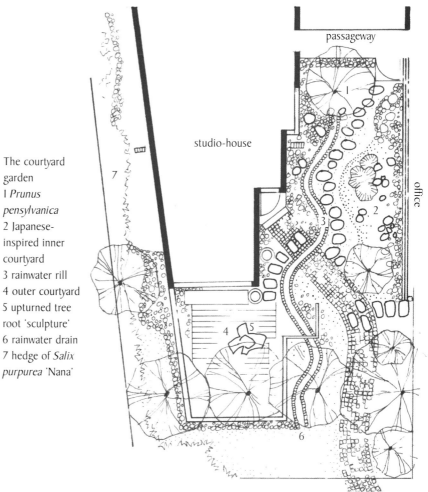

The courtyard garden
1 *Prunus pensylvanica*
2 Japanese-inspired inner courtyard
3 rainwater rill
4 outer courtyard
5 upturned tree root 'sculpture'
6 rainwater drain
7 hedge of *Salix purpurea* 'Nana'

passageway

studio-house

office

ABOVE Virtue was made of necessity in the small courtyard between the architect's studio-house (left) and office building (right). The curving lines of the stone and gravel path, areas of cobblestones and a clever backcloth of plants broaden the narrow garden space. The focal point here, close to the side door, is a beautiful small hardy tree, the pin cherry (*Prunus pensylvanica*), whose bark blends perfectly with the slanting timber of the house walls.

RIGHT Though the silver birch, whose bark matches the warm brown timbers of the studio and passage so perfectly, reminds us that we are in Finland, this contemplative garden with its soft lines and beautiful details is inspired by Japanese models.

LEFT Horizontal patterns in the simple blockwork wall and timber floor panels contrast with the clear-stemmed trunk of the birch in the outer courtyard. A tree root sculpture spreads out over a carpet of *Vinca minor* and asarabacca (*Asarum europaeum*). The Italian honeysuckle (*Lonicera caprifolium*) clings to the wall at right.
BELOW The curving water channel that carries rainwater from the tripartite roofs makes a pretty feature among the varied textures of stone that create a harmony of colour and form against the low green planting.

Virtue was made of necessity in this small garden, an area of a mere 115 square metres (137 square yards). The wavy lines of the water channel and gravel area and the curve of the paved main path broaden out the space with its clever backcloth of plants. The focal point of the small courtyard close to the side door is a beautiful little hardy tree with a green trunk and white stripes. It is the pin cherry (*Prunus pensylvanica*), whose large tri-palmate lanced leaves change colour later in the autumn to palest light yellow. Beautiful red autumnal colouring is also provided by the shrub *Spiraea betulifolia*, planted as a dense group at the entrance to the garden. The different structures of the stones, paving and gravel form a contrast with a peaceful flower bed with plants giving good ground cover such as *Waldsteinia ternata*, saxifrage (*Saxifraga* x *arendsii*), Dwarf

Bearded irises and thyme (*Thymus serpyllum*) together with a green cushion of moss on stones. Individual taller groups of perennials, ferns and shrubs are accentuated features standing out from this green, gently dynamic and on the whole horizontal area of plants: the Siberian iris (*Iris sibirica*), lady's mantle (*Alchemilla mollis*), elephant's ears (*Bergenia cordifolia*), *Rodgersia aesculifolia*, the ostrich fern (*Matteuccia struthiopteris*) and shrubs such as the dwarf Russian almond (*Prunus tenella*) and a few small pines. It is a small, contemplative garden, inspired by Japanese models and with soft lines and beautiful details with plants, stones and a paved area, a garden whose small size should be forgotten, which is just what Pekka Salminen intended.

Although Japanese garden culture, which is rooted in

RIGHT Behind the two buildings is a raised timber fence which, with its low view through to the lawn and birches of the next-door garden, allows a feeling of openness to prevail. At the same time the buildings and side path are screened at eye level. Beneath the birch trees, pink-flowering *Rubus odoratus* forms the main planting.

religion and Asian philosophy and traditions, is alien to this nordic country, there are scenes on the Schären Islands with stunted pines and picturesque rocks that are reminiscent of Japanese landscapes. And the abundance of mosses there is enough to turn even the Japanese green with envy.

Walls of grey concrete blocks (also used inside the house) form a small outer courtyard, just 23 metres (27 yards) square close to the studio's main entrance. It is enlivened by a silver birch and *Hosta lancifolia*, saxifrage (*Saxifraga rotundifolia*), the plume poppy (*Macleaya cordata*), an herbaceous plant with blue-green decorative leaves that grows up to 3 metres (10 feet) tall, provide further accents. The climbing Italian honeysuckle (*Lonicera caprifolium*) provides wall cover, and an upturned tree root from the wilds of Finland forms a sculpture.

The boundary of the narrow third garden situated behind the two buildings, just 88 square metres (105 square yards) in size, is marked by a wooden fence 'on stilts', an unusual solution that provides a screen at eye level whereas the lower open half, a metre (3 feet) high, allows an unimpeded view of the lawn and other birch trees in the neighbouring garden, a vista which extends its narrow space. This garden begins as a passage, with concrete paving stones and contrasting pebbles behind the black wooden house, and finishes as a small terrace with reddish-brown, hard-baked bricks behind the studio where hydrangeas and *Clematis alpina* climb. In spring, shrubs such as Korean forsythia (*F. ovata*) and Allegheny serviceberry (*Amelanchier laevis*) flower, while in summer there are perennials such as astilbe, plantain lilies and delphiniums.

A Walk Through
The Scandinavian Garden

A key to understanding the garden in Scandinavia lies in its close relationship to the landscape: they are like microscosm and macrocosm, locked in a constantly alternating dialogue. A walk through the gardens shown in the book would reveal unexpected approaches to organizing the space available, such as the wide variety of geometric and organic shapes used in garden composition. The choice of materials, hard structures and planting, is conditioned by the harshness of the winter and by what the geology and topography of the area yield.

Our senses are stimulated by the particular combinations of shape and colour; by the care taken to mix fragility and solidity in the structures and planting; by the relationship of the garden with its surroundings and with the intimacy of the house; and by the manner in which even the smallest corner may be brought to life, perhaps by a piece of topiary or a coloured stone. These are all different aspects of the garden; taken together they produce an abundance of riches and surprises.

The biggest differences are between the north and south, bearing in mind that southern Scandinavia is already part of northern Europe. The garden in its most formal and elaborate state is to be found in Denmark and the south of Sweden, where a flat, gently undulating countryside allows more freedom in the choice of form and composition. Once the mountains of Hallandsåsen have been crossed the countryside hardens, the climate dictates a sharp distinction between winter and summer and the gardens take on a more subdued aspect. Moving north, the hills, mountains and rocks, the natural vegetation and the wide stretches of water predominate with such emotive power that they tower over the artificial construct of the garden as if to say there were no need of such a thing.

Although the design and construction of Scandinavian gardens differ according to latitude and its limitations on the range of plants grown, we find that this is not necessarily the most immediate impression given; rather, it is the garden's

harmonious presence in the landscape, and the designer's respect for the natural surroundings, that makes the modern Scandinavian approach to garden design both sympathetic and inspired.

Another factor contributing to garden design stems from the Scandinavian character, which tends to be much more open than we might expect of a people from the North. They have a high degree of social awareness, but at the same time are mindful of their own and others' individuality, maintaining a fine balance between simplicity and formality, both in matters of design and in their dealings with one another. In Sweden, thanks to the *Allemandsrätten* law, it is perfectly possible to cross private property and pitch a tent for one night, even if one does not know the owner of the land. There is no risk of being threatened by shotguns or pursued by snarling dogs as happens in other countries. The concept of ownership is less imperious here than, say, in Italy or the south of France where high walls, thorny hedges and entrance gates ensure that your view and passage are restricted. Instead, boundary fences are almost non-existent. You must be discreet, but crossing land is not seen as an intrusion and if you come across the owner it is quite likely that an invitation to drink a cup of coffee together and a discussion on the beauty of a particular flower will follow. And as the marks on their hands show, it is with rare exceptions the owners themselves who hoe the soil, dig the holes, plant the trees and bushes, do the pruning and construct the paths, pergolas and fencing, because they enjoy it and because hiring labour is costly.

There is, however, great competition to lay out the most beautiful garden or find the most ingenious solution to a

OPPOSITE As an example of the 'artifice' of planting, roses at Rosendal Barony, at the Hardanger fjord, Norway, contrast strikingly with the natural grandeur.

ABOVE The gardens at Hvitträsk, west of Helsinki, combine tall verticals with low rounded forms, such as these trees and pillars and a gently curving lawn within a circular path. Solid granite forms are contrasted with light and airy trellis constructions. BELOW The Japanese garden within the Ronneby park, designed jointly by Sven-Ingvar Andersson and Akira Mochizuki. The framing of the woodland from the timber pavilion brings it sharply into focus, deepening one's awareness of a forest 'experience'.

problem. Contributing to the flowering of new ideas are the various festivals, which are traditionally organized in Copenhagen and more recently in Stockholm, and in different nurseries such as Hammenhög in Sweden. These delight the interested visitor and offer examples of the ingenuity and sometimes irony of garden design and artefacts.

The Scandinavians have always deeply loved their woods: the intense feeling generated by their vertical structures may almost amount to a primitive form of religion. Nevertheless, to make way for a garden, the woodland often has to be cut back to fringe a clearing and allow sunlight in – the indispensable element of a more varied life. In the forest of Småland, Sweden, Sten Dunér carves out space in the grand manner, making architectural counterpoints between the wooden houses, which, together with his often incidental art forms such as coloured stones or sculptural glass balls, allow his poetic vision to unfold in a totally original blend of ancient tradition and philosophical premise (see pages 48–54).

Alvar Aalto's experimental holiday house in the forest of Muuratsalo, Finland, was born of different principles. The house and inner courtyard lie on a rocky promontory which juts out into a lake, and the irregular lines of the building fit between one tree trunk and another. The house interior opens out solely onto a square courtyard which is enclosed by high brick walls plastered white on the outside. On one side of the

LEFT Alvar Aalto's holiday house lies unobtrusively on a rocky promontory. The imposing verticals of the trees contrast with the angular planes of the low, white-washed walls which they interrupt and so control.

RIGHT Dancing and playing bronze figures, including three 'Musician Angels' (1952) and a 'Head of Orpheus' in the Carl Milles sculpture garden, Stockholm. The tall supporting columns that echo the pine trees extend out from the woodland edge as if into a sunlit glade.

courtyard, which has an open-air fireplace, thin wooden posts support climbing plants to reproduce the structure of the forest.

Moss-covered rocks and stone boulders among trees bring to mind images of the Japanese landscape, and it is not surprising that the gardens of the Far East arouse much interest in Scandinavia. We can inhale the atmosphere of the Land of the Rising Sun at Ronneby park where Sven Ingvar Andersson together with the Japanese landscape architect Akira Mochizuki created a Japanese garden area as a sensory experience. In the beechwoods, which they left intact, are several elements that recall the Japanese garden, among them a wooden pavilion built directly over the bare earth, from where one can absorb the magical spectacle of the sun's rays brushing gently against the leaves and trunks of the trees.

The feeling for the woods is so deep-rooted in the Scandinavian psyche that, even when they are absent, there is a tendency to recreate them. The delicate statues set precariously on a series of thin columns in Carl Milles' garden at Stockholm, today a museum, bring to mind the slender poles of larch or birch, or other trees that are most commonly found in the Scandinavian countries. In Denmark, where since medieval times large wooded areas have been largely eliminated in order to make way for cultivation, tall deciduous trees – lime, ash, beech and oak – predominate, due mainly to the mildness of climate occasioned by the proximity of the sea, which is never

more than 50 kilometres (20 miles) from the hinterland.

The situation is similar in the Swedish province of Skåne where elm disease, which has ravaged this most beautiful of trees on the Continent for decades, only arrived in the last twenty years. In the garden the elms were normally placed together with the hedges to form a wind barrier around isolated houses. Occasionally present in the more southerly zones, birch becomes the most common of the deciduous trees as we move north where, together with different types of service tree, it mingles with the great pine forests. The *Salix alba* var. *sericea* of Canadian origin has found Scandinavian conditions to its liking and helps to brighten up the landscape.

In Denmark and southern Sweden tall hedges enclose the garden and mark out clearly defined spaces, acting as essential protection from the wind which blows forcefully for most of the year. At three to four metres (10 to 16 feet) high, they afford protection so that flower beds can be cultivated safe from the risk that petals might be damaged by sudden gusts of wind. Hedges are also distinctive features of areas under cultivation, as points of reference amid a network of seemingly identical roads and lanes. Scattered among them, apple, pear and cherry trees yield a covering of white flowers in spring.

In certain areas it is hawthorn, beech, box, yew and privet that are most commonly used to create these clearly recognizable green barriers. Farther north, rhododendron,

LEFT ABOVE At the Agenippe Fountain in Millesgården, Lidingö, outside Stockholm, bronze youths, each representing one of the arts, are inspired by the goddess Agenippe. They run and leap in unison with spouting dolphins. The graceful curving arcs of water and the ripples on the pond add to the movement. The sculptor Carl Milles created two versions of this work: the other is the Fountain of the Muses at Brooke Green sculpture gardens in South Carolina.

LEFT BELOW Standing as steady as two tree trunks, these scarecrow-sculptures with weasel heads enliven rows of salad vegetables at a garden festival at Rosendal Park in Stockholm, in summer 1998.

RIGHT A group of cockerels sculpted in box under Himalayan birches (*Betula utilis*) in Otto Wiese's garden in Skåne, Sweden, are another example of the irony to be found in the Scandinavian garden.

RIGHT A vertical screen of woven willow branches, the rediscovery of an old tradition, shown at the Rosendal exhibition in Stockholm (1998) is a good example of the light fencing that eschews privacy for a more 'transparent' boundary.

service tree and Mugo pine are more widespread as hedges because their tough keratinous leaves, or in some cases needles, expose a smaller surface area to low temperatures. One surprise is the presence of lilac (*Syringa vulgaris*) which is able to prosper in climates varying from the Mediterranean to the rigours of Oslo. Hawthorn (or whitethorn, *Crataegus*) grows wild but is also much used in gardens because it requires little work. Left unclipped, its white flowers give out a delightful scent in late spring while in autumn their colourful berries light up the garden and provide a cornucopia for the birds. Beech (*Fagus*) leaves turn from green to a golden copper colour which may then become deepest red if the rigours of winter arrive unannounced, while the trunks and branches of the hornbeams are clearly visible through their dry leaves which remain until spring. Box (*Buxus*), a familiar presence in the rural garden and in the cemetery, grows well in heavy soil but develops even more slowly than in southern Europe as it is not resistant to very harsh winters; it is, we might say, almost an indicator of more southerly climes. It is trained into spheres or, grown as low hedging in a simple rectangular shape, serves as a border to the beds that are in flower for just a few months. Yew (*Taxus*), the plant most commonly associated with the art of topiary, is

moulded into shapes here as well, an example being the bestiary of Videbehus, the work of the sculptor and landscape designer Junggreen Have in a park designed by C.Th. Sørensen. It is commonplace in Denmark to give sculptured hedges an undulation that fosters optical illusions and allows the sun's rays to create different combinations of light and shadow, as for instance in Torben Schønherr's lakeside garden (pages 86–91). Privet (*Ligustrum*) is widely used, especially *L. vulgare* 'Atrovirens', an evergreen that is resistant to the cold. It may be combined with different types of bush in order to introduce some colour to a winter garden.

Also in Denmark, Sørensen and his school have often

ABOVE The yew bestiary of Videbehus in Denmark, a hedge sculpture by Junggreen Have. From the midst of an outer circle, like a green millipede that hobbles slowly along, wrapped around itself, emerges a collection of mythical birds, bears and tortoises, their outlines sharpened by the contrasting colour of the yellow leaves shed by the surrounding beech trees in autumn.

OPPOSITE Graphic colour in a garden designed by Junggreen Have at the ancient Loegum Kloster in Denmark, now used as a conference centre. The long lines of closely clipped autumnal beech hedges alternate with grass paths and granite edgings, but are relieved by light-hearted topiary blocks of dark green yew.

LEFT, ABOVE & RIGHT At the garden colony at Naerum, Denmark, C.Th. Sørensen enclosed each garden with an oval hedge. When seen from the air, the forty-eight small gardens and houses situated on uneven terrain look like a cluster of cells viewed through a microscope. Their common form but individual content is fascinating to witness, as are the grassy areas that one can walk around in between them – myriad spaces constantly in flux.

designed hedges that describe a circle or an ellipse, in a conscious refusal to allow axial lines to predominate, but rather to favour a convergence on a central core or two fundamental points. These closed shapes dispense with acute angles that disturb the eye, in a search for that perfect equilibrium which the Chinese developed in their gardens.

The circular form has deep-rooted origins in the Scandinavian countries. Many archaeological discoveries at Viking sites have uncovered this form or the more elongated, elliptical boat-shape. It was usual, in earlier times, for Danish village elders to form a circle in the forest in order to administer justice. There are many examples of the circular form still in use. Sørensen inserted one high up in a solid stone wall separating a garden and its lawn from the sea; the circle opens up a telescopic vista of the water's flickering light, enriching the garden with an entirely unexpected dimension. In his last project, the design for his daughter Sonja's garden (pages 126–9), a circular form was excavated from the soil; if it is assumed that the lawn represents zero on a vertical axis, we can say that this form occupies 'negative' space, like a minus value on a temperature scale. In a garden at Herning in Jutland, by introducing a succession of hedges of different shapes and heights, he sought to transpose to the garden the musical experience of high and low notes.

Transformed into an ellipse, the circular form becomes a key feature of landscape design in the garden colony designed by C.Th. Sørensen at Naerum. Here, elliptical hedges separate the gardens where occupants have their own individual space and can delight in forming a garden, yet the whole forms a work of art, which visitors walking on the grass paths can appreciate.

OPPOSITE CENTRE A kitchen garden designed by Simon Irvine at Tomarps Gård near Kristianstad, Sweden, is composed of spiral segments that come together in a circular form. Green vegetables alternate with cutting flowers. Irvine, an Englishman who has lived in Sweden for a number of years, has designed various gardens around the country.

OPPOSITE BOTTOM Stylized straw figures created by the Swedish sculptress Ulla Viotti evoke the ancient tradition of the wise men gathered in a circle in the woods. Straw 'baskets' similar to these figures were used by fishermen to catch eels.

RIGHT C.Th. Sørensen's sea wall opening called 'the moon door' in on the *strandvejen* between Copenhagen and Helsingør.

RIGHT Artist Brigitta Stenberg used terracotta pots to form a circle of concentric rings in tall grass, like a fossil shell on the lawn, for a summer exhibition at Hammenhög nursery between Ystad and Simrishamn, Sweden, in 1997.

ABOVE The round shape of this garden comes from the base of a former oil storage cistern. Bruno Richter transformed it into a roof garden 7 metres (22 feet) above street level for the inhabitants of an apartment building in Gothenburg, Sweden.
BELOW A water staircase at the Rudolf Steiner College at Ytterjärna, near Stockholm. The movement of the water through each basin ensures that it remains clear and pure.

Where protection from the wind is not a priority, gardens are often surrounded by low or unobtrusive fencing which serves to delimit the property but leaves the view open for anyone passing to enjoy. The fences may be made with small vertical poles interwoven with willow branches, or by post and rail fencing left natural or painted in different colours. Throughout Scandinavia low dry-stone walls and hard surfacing in gardens are almost always composed of rounded granite blocks or cobbles (a tradition from the courtyards of old farms or castles); they declare the unchanging solidity of the Nordic world.

A different use of solid form is evident in the 'garden' of Hvitträsk, west of Helsinki, designed around his studio house by Eliel Saarinen (1873–1950), one of the most important Finnish architects of the early twentieth century, and worked on together with his friends and colleagues Herman Gesellius and Armas Lindgren. The garden has a front facing the wood which descends towards a lake (see page 170), from where a visible wall of large boulders supports the imposing edifice. The rest of the garden is on a higher level and embraces the building on three sides. A similar sense of solidity is emitted in the garden which the landscape designer Bruno Richter created at Gothenburg using the circular base of an oil storage cistern. In an interesting salvage operation, he brought together granite rocks, on which the city is built, the new garden and the living area to which it is joined by a footbridge that calls to mind the gangplank used by ferryboats. Similar rocky formations are to be found in Oslo and Helsinki, the testimony of a very ancient glaciation that did not experience earthquakes.

It has been remarked that water, whether in the form of sea, lake or river, is an ever-present feature of the Scandinavian landscape. Like the forest, water is buried deep in the collective subconscious of the people, experienced both as challenge and diversion, a symbol of the fluidity of life, and an enchantment. One especially original idea was presented by Annika Oskarson and Thomas Nordström at the exhibition held in the Rosendal Park at Stockholm in 1998.

In the gardens of the hinterland water appears in the form of small lakes or basins where water lilies swim and aquatic plants grow, or as a biotope used as a stopping off place by passing birds; it is very rarely in motion. But by contrast strong jets of

OPPOSITE Annika Oskarson and Thomas Nordström's water installation at the garden festival at Rosendal Park, Stockholm. From a mirror-like expanse of completely still water, a series of rounded forms, covered in moss and pierced at the centre, exhaled intermittent puffs of white smoke.

water do enliven some large public spaces such as the canal port of Stockholm, and the parks of Copenhagen, Oslo and Helsinki. In Millesgården, a sculpture park, little jets spurt from the statues, rippling the surface of the water in which the figures are reflected (see page 172). In smaller gardens, however, water does not usually have a key role to play because of the difficulty of its management in a harsh climate, where ponds are converted to ice, pipes freeze, fountains remain empty and fish and plants go into their long hibernation.

The images created by the long, cold winter carry a distinct emotional feel: leafless trees still burdened with apples at Christmas; berries half-hidden by a crystalline blanket but standing out against the whiteness to remind us that there is a garden under there somewhere. In the cocoon-like silence, we could almost forget the ubiquitous birch if it were not for the other trees that allow them to stand out in contrast.

The fences, usually simple affairs, become crenellated walls, like new and hitherto undiscovered structures. And as the snow melts, a range of interesting patterns becomes visible, created by the wooden posts and the interwoven branches that bind them together, leaving space enough for a fleeting glimpse of the outside world, of the interplay of light and shadow.

Finally there are the flowers, those fleeting protagonists of the countryside that create magical moments of colour and whose selection and planting is the subject of endless winter conversations. The blooming of the flowers is eagerly awaited and follows a calendar which, while always repeated, is not tied strictly to the passing of the months but varies from year to year. It calls to mind the book by Karl Foerster (1874–1970), which divides the year into further seasons, according to when 'signal' plants that herald a change first appear. Foerster was a German nursery gardener and hybrid cultivator who in the 1930s exercised a great influence on garden composition, pioneering the use of perennial plants, ferns and grasses.

The first flower to appear at the end of winter, while the fields are still covered with patches of snow, is the aconite (*Eranthis hyemalis*), suddenly creating carpets of yellow a little before the snowdrops emerge. Then *Leucojum vernum* peeps

LEFT Apples left hanging on branches as the first snow of winter arrives.
RIGHT: TOP Snow piled high against a wall with a ceramic piece of sculpture by Ulla Viotti in her garden in Österlen.
CENTRE Hips of the wild dog rose (*Rosa canina*).
BOTTOM A low winter sun shines on blackened rhododendron leaves with their caps of frozen snow.

ABOVE Aconites (*Eranthis hyemalis*) peep through melting
snow, the first hint that spring is on its way.
BELOW Tall white daisies (*Leucanthemum vulgare*) and the lawn
daisy *Bellis perennis* arrive just before the dandelions that
always manage to disguise themselves among them.
OPPOSITE Blossom time with apple trees and myriad dandelion
clocks in Sven-Ingvar Andersson's garden.

through with its tiny white bells and yellow or greenish tips, together with the red of *Petasites hybridus* in humid areas, this being more common than the *P. albus* that is found in Karen Blixen's garden. *Hepatica nobilis* sprouts in the woods with its fine violet petals, and hot on its heels follows *Anemone nemorosa*, brightening the atmosphere with its white flowers. These are the first signs of the impending spring which bursts on the scene suddenly but much later than in other European countries, and which coincides with the opening of the beech buds, firstly in Denmark and then in the south of Sweden.

Later, the fields become covered in white daisies (*Bellis perennis*), followed by the yellow of dandelions (*Taraxacum officinale)*, until white takes over again as they go to seed at the same time as the fruit trees come into blossom.

In June, fields of wheat, barley and oats are stained with red and blue as the poppies and cornflowers (*Centaurea cyanus*) come into flower. Abundance at its peak is celebrated with the festival of *midsommar* in Sweden, and that of *Sankt Hans* in Denmark, around 21 June, when the sun is at its highest point. This is the most joyous moment of the year and a veritable kaleidoscope of colour.

Between the end of July and the beginning of August, the raspberry and blackcurrant bushes that grow both in the wild and in the cultivated garden are heavy with fruit, providing raw material for the tasty jams that accompany so many dishes in Nordic cuisine. The best summers are hot and sunny, but there are wetter years when sun and rain alternate several times during the day. Towards the end of August, the leaves start to fall, the temperature to drop and summer vanishes in a flash.

There are several different approaches to the choice of cultivated flowers. One draws inspiration more directly from nature and makes use of wild plants, but the tradition of the English cottage garden with its bright array of summer flowers is also popular. However, the artists' gardens are a thing apart, capable of taking their cue from the strangest places and achieving particularly original and evocative compositions. There are also many gardens with beautiful plants, put together in the tradition of the dedicated collector such as Carl von Linné but these are often to the detriment of the overall design.

The sunlight is much more subdued than in Latin countries and allows for the creation of delicate pairings that are conspicuous even when the sky is grey. Shapes and colours are generally considered not simply in relation to each other but also in relation to the houses. Outside the urban areas the buildings are almost all constructed in wood, from the typical

house with vertical panelling whose colour can vary from a rusty red to mustard yellow, sometimes even an icy blue, its windows and doors painted white, to the indispensable sauna. This results in combinations of rare elegance. In the Norwegian village of Vaterland, near Frederikstad, the blue flowers of delphiniums stand out against a background of rust-coloured and dull grey wooden beams, while climbing roses mount the perforated wood façades. In the Finnish countryide near Ruoversi, the dark red houses are in perfect harmony with the crimson pink of epilobium, while the orange and white lilies complement the appearance of the white window frames.

The chance to enjoy the warmth of the sun, and the flowers and plants in all their glory, is a pleasure which lasts for so short a time that it is exploited to the fullest extent. When creating their gardens, Scandinavian gardeners generally seek the most favourable micro-climatic conditions in order to risk planting species that would not otherwise survive. At the same time, they will avoid causing great upheaval to the topography, for they

respect what nature has provided. The houses extend into the gardens, as if they were open-air rooms where every detail is studied with care and imagination. The most sheltered corner is always reserved for mealtimes, and often indicated by the presence of a large umbrella which is kept closed by day but in the evening helps to protect against the humidity.

To extend the season, there is widespread use of gazebos and garden pavilions, and particularly what the Swedes call the *lust-hus*, a polygonal glass-windowed arbour fitted out with

ABOVE Four painted wood façades in the village of Vaterland, south of Oslo. Pink and red pelargoniums, purple aubrieta and yellow pansies in white window boxes stand out against buff panels; fresh green foliage and a blue delphinium frame a smiling painted face among the greys, whites and browns of doors and walls; bright red and creamy roses decorate grey panelling; and pink-red roses and white daisies stand out against lilac-grey doors.

OPPOSITE White and orange lilies with purple violas and daisies (*Leucanthemum vulgare*) in the courtyard of an old farmhouse near Ruoversi in Finland.

chairs or benches, and a table with candles to be lit when family or friends get together to eat a meal or take coffee and biscuits. Sven-Ingvar Andersson has a particularly fine example (pages 18–19). These arbours allow one to experience the sensation of being in the garden, even if it is raining, and may be used until the first cold weather arrives; then it is necessary to abandon them and shut oneself away in the warmth of the house. At the Rudolf Steiner College at Ytterjärna, near Stockholm, a thatched pavilion stands at the edge of the lake. Outside it is painted an ultramarine blue, dark at the bottom and lightening towards the top. The inner part (see front of jacket) has been glassed in to provide a protective place. It is a blend of blue, grey and white, like a whisper of violet: the colours react to their surroundings with the same sensitivity as water, sky and light.

In a sheltered area, we may find another small glass structure, the greenhouse proper. Here, with the attention given to a new-born child, people will cultivate small tomato plants for the pleasure of having a fresh salad, a few vines for the joy of producing a bunch of grapes, perhaps some hot peppers or sweet basil. These are all plants that could not be grown outside and to succeed in cultivating them becomes a matter of pride, an indication of real green fingers.

A characteristic of Nordic peoples, and in particular of their garden lovers, is a detestation of the noise that is so typical of Latin countries. They show a preference for being meditative, or contemplative – tendencies evident in the many gardens where chairs, benches, or small settees may be placed in quiet and especially pleasing spots. One can sit to read a book, indulge in friendly chatter, or simply look at the countryside.

ABOVE The thatched pavilion, a place for meditation or contemplation at the Rudolf Steiner College, faces the lake, beyond a pond edged with silver willows. Constructed of pine and fir timbers and glass it was designed by Arne Klingborg and built by Torsten Grindal.
OPPOSITE The peace of early morning in a scene straight out of our grandmothers' time. The sides of the pavilion, which was designed by Jan-Erik Nordborg for Harriet Hägle's garden near Helsingborg, can be removed for winter. Barely visible against the light, the rose 'Kiftsgate' grows over the pavilion roof. In the foreground are white *Campanula alliariifolia*, the violet of *C. carpatica* and the yellow heads of *Achillea filipendulina*. Next to the pavilion stands an elegant *Acer palmatum* with the rose 'Pink Grootendorst' behind.
FOLLOWING PAGE The seat at the boundary of Lulu Salto's garden, situated to the north of Copenhagen.

Bibliography

Akerblom, Petter, *Gestalta med mossa* [*Structuring with Moss*], Stad & Land, Agricultural University of Sweden, Ålnarp, 1987

Andersson, Sven-Ingvar & Høyer, Steen, *C.Th. Sørensen - en havekunstner*, Arkitektens Forlag, Copenhagen, 1993

Berglund, Karin, *Lust och fägring*, Rabén Prisma, Stockholm, 2nd ed. 1994

Dunér, Sten, *Trädgårdar: Bilder mellan idé och verklighet*, Gidlunds, Stockholm, 1984

Essen, Madeleine von, *Hager Til Lyst Og Nytte*, Chr. Schibsteds Forlag A/S, Oslo, 1997

Freud, Sigmund, 'Das Unheimliche' in *Sigmund Freud, Gesammelte Werke*, (chronologisch geordnet, *Zwölfter Band, Werke aus dem Jahren 1917-1920*, pp. 228-268, herausgegeben von Anna Freud), Imago Publishing Co., London, repr. 1955

Goode, Patrick, Jellicoe, Geoffrey and Susan, & Lancaster, Michael, *The Oxford Companion to Gardens*, Oxford University Press, 1991

Hauxner, Malene, *Fantasiens Have*, Arkitektens Forlag, Copenhagen, 1993

Hilliers' Manual of Trees & Shrubs, David & Charles Publishers Ltd, Newton Abbot, 1997

Irvine, Simon, *Om Trädgårdar*, Bokförlaget Prisma, Stockholm, 1998

Lagerlöf, Selma, *Nils Holgerssons underbara resa genom Sverige*, Albert Bonniers Förlag, Stockholm, 1907

Luciani, Domenico & Latini, Luigi (eds) *Scandinavia. Luoghi, figure, gesti di una civiltà del paesaggio*, Edizioni Fondazione Benetton Studi Ricerche/Canova, Treviso, 1998

Lund, Annemarie, *Guide Til Dansk havekunst år 1000-1996* [*Guide to Danish landscape architecture 1000-1996*], Arkitektens Forlag, Copenhagen, 1997

Molin, Ulla, *Leva Med Trädgård*, Förlag AB Wiken, Sweden, 1986

Möller, Lotte, *Trädgårdens natur*, Bonniers Förlag, Stockholm, 1992

Möller, Lotte, *Maryhill: en trädgård i Lund*, Bonniers Förlag, Stockholm, 1994

Salto Stephensen, Lulu, *Tradition og Fornyelse i Dansk Havekunst*, Forlag Frangi Pani, Denmark, 1993

Samuel, Richard, *Novalis Schriften, Zweiter Band, Die Werke Friedrich von Hardenbergs, Das Philosphische Werk I*, W. Kohlhammer Verlag, Stuttgart, 1965

Samuelsson, Lars Eric & Schenkmanis, Ulf, *Trädgårdstips för hela året*, Natur och Kultur, Stockholm, 1997

Schama, Simon, *Landscape & Memory*, Fontana Press, London, 1996

Schenk, George, *Moss Gardening: including lichens, liverworts & other miniatures*, Timber Press Publications, Portland, 1997

Skaarer, Nils, *Elleville Hager, 40 hager for enhver smag* [*40 ideas for gardens*], (includes intro. on moss gardens, pp. 140-143), Landbruksforlaget, Oslo, 1998

Sørensen, C.Th., *Haver-Tanker og arbejder*, Christian Eilers Forlag, København, 1975

[var. authors], *Tilegnet Sven-Ingvar Andersson*, Arkitektens Forlag, Copenhagen, 1994

KAREN BLIXEN

Andersson, S.-I., Hertel, L., Lasson, F. & Rasmussen, S. E., *Karen Blixen's Flowers, nature and art at Rungstedlund*, Christian Eilers Publishers, Copenhagen 1992

Karen Blixen Museet, Rungstedlund [texts by Karen Blixen, Frans Lasson and Steen Eiler Rasmussen], pub. 1991 by the Museum

Vestergaard, Gunver, *Nye Buketter fra Karen Blixens have* [*New Bouquets from Karen Blixen's Garden*], ch. by Andreas Brunn, 'Rungstedlunds have og herligheder' ['The Garden at Rungstedlund and its Splendours'] Haveselskabet, the Danish Royal Horticultural Society, Lyngby, Denmark, 1995

The text of Chief Seattle (Sealth)'s speech, 1854 (p. 111) is taken from the Internet

EDVARD GRIEG

Benestad, Finn & Schjelderup-Ebbe, Dag, *Edvard Grieg; mennesket og kunstneren*, H. Aschehoug & Co., 1980 [trans. W. H. Halverson & L. B. Sateren, *Edvard Grieg: The man and the Artist*, University of Nebraska Press/AlanSutton, Gloucester, 1988

Horton, John, *Grieg (Master Musicians Series)*, J.M. Dent Ltd, London, 1976

Krellmann, Hanspeter, *Edvard Grieg*, Rowohlt Taschenbuch Verlag, Hamburg, 1999

[var. authors] '*Dein Grieg*' (Catalogue of the Jubilee Exhibition on the occasion of the 150th anniversary of the birth of Edvard Grieg, at the West Norway Museum of Applied Art, Bergen, 29 April to 3 October 1993), Bergen, 1993

The Gardens and their Designers

DENMARK
p. 20   *Fields, flax & clipped hedgerows* designer Sven Hansen; owner & garden plan Erik Heide

p. 88   *Flowing lawns & beech hedges* garden design & plan by Torben Schønherr

p. 106   *Karen Blixen's 'Place of Bliss'* owner Rungstedlund Foundation

p. 126   *Oval in a triangle* designers C.Th. Sørensen (garden plan)/Sonja Poll (owner)

p. 147   *Geometry in yellow & green* designer/owner & plan Andreas Brunn

p. 176   *Allotment gardens at Naerum* design & plan C.Th. Sørensen

FINLAND
p. 56   *Rocks, mosses & berries* designer/owner & plan Tom Simons

p. 66   *Alvar Aalto's Villa Mairea*: owner Mairea Foundation; design & *garden plan* Alvar Aalto

p. 162   *Pekka Salminen's studio & garden* garden design & plan Gretel Hemgård

NORWAY
p. 26   *Rock outcrop with flowers & pines* designers/owners Olav & Grethe Li

p. 62   *Nature garden among the fields* designer/owner Nils Skaarer

p. 72   *Green hillside with stone paths* garden designed by Torborg Frölich; house by Kaare Frölich (owners)

p. 76   *Fables, yellow & gold* designer Egil Gabrielsen; plan Mette Eggen

p. 116   *Edvard Grieg's 'Hill of the Trolls'* owner Grieg Foundation

SWEDEN
p. 14   *Fairy-tale grove in box & hawthorn* designer/owner & plan Sven-Ingvar Andersson

p. 30   *Trees, banks, wild planting & water* designer/owner Karl-Dietrich Bühler

p. 40   *Sky & heath* designer/owner & plan Per Friberg

p. 44   *Triangular tapestry* designers/owners Barbara Johnson & Botvid Kihlman

p. 48   *Romantic glades in summerland* designer/owner Sten Dunér

p. 92   *Lakeside flower border* designer/owner Helena Emanuelsson

p. 100   *Wind, waves & cliffs* designer Håkan Lundberg

p. 112   *Seashore rock garden* designer Helge Lundström

p. 130   *Spheres, parallels & garden rooms* designer/owner Bertil Hansson

p. 140   *Courtyard garden in green & blue* designer/owner Tommy Nordström

p. 152   *Wildwood, flowers & mountain plants* designers/owners Eva & Roland Gustavsson

p. 158   *Exotic courtyard with pink & gold* designer/owner Karin Wassberg

Index

Aalto, Alvar and Aino 10, 66-71, 162

Abraham, Dr Max 120

Acaena buchananii (New Zealand burr) 134

Acer (maple); Japanese maple 130, 135
 callipes 139
 negundo 46
 palmatum 187
 pseudoplatanus (sycamore) 48, 51
 rufinerve (snake-bark maple) 152

Achillea filipendulina 187

aconite, winter (*Eranthis hyemalis*) 181, 182

Aconitum napellus 51, 56, 95, 128

Actinidia kolomikta 68, 140, 153

Agapanthus (African lily) 22, 46, 145

Ailanthus altissima 142, 143

Alchemilla mollis 36, 39, 95, 139, 156, 166

alder 72, 75, 92

Alisma (water plantain) 38

alkanet (*Anchusa azurea*) 99

Allium 14, 16, 110

almond, Russian (*Prunus tenella*) 166

Alnus (alder) 92; *incana* (grey alder) 72, 75

alpine garden 135, 136

Amelanchier
 canadensis (shadbush) 64

 laevis (Allegheny serviceberry) 148, 167
 spicata (juneberry) 65, 153, 156

Ammophila arenaria (marram grass) 114

Anchusa azurea (alkanet) 99

Andersen, Hans Christian 91, 108

Andersson, Sven-Ingvar 4, 9, 14-18, 111, 170-1, 187

Anemone 108
 hupehensis 156
 nemerosa 139, 152, 182
 ranunculoides 152

Anethum graveolens (dill) 22

Antennaria (cat's ears) 152

Anthriscus sylvestris (cow parsley) 114

apple 54, 64, 90-1, 104, 126-8, 171, 181

Aquilegia (columbine) 14, 95, 156

Araucaria araucana (monkey puzzle) 160

archangel, yellow (*Lamium galeobdolon*) 75

Arctostaphylos uva-ursi (bearberry) 28

Armeria maritima (sea thrift) 65, 112, 114

Artemisia (mugwort) 46, 134
 stelleriana 34
 vulgaris 114

artichoke, ornamental 20, 21

arum lily *see Zantedeschia*

Asarum europaeum (asarabacca, wild ginger) 39, 135, 139, 156, 166
ash *see Sorbus*
Asmussen, Marianne Wirenfeldt 108
Äspönas 44-7
Aster 64, 65
    alpinum 65
    amellus 'King George' 145
    dumosus 'Schneekissen' 145
Astilbe 64, 73, 94-5, 99, 167
Astilboides tabularis 136, 139
Astrantia major (masterwort) 94-5, 128, 135
Athyrium niponicum var. *pictum* 135
Aubrieta 184
Azalea 75
baby blue-eyes (*Nemophila menziesii*) 99
bachelor's buttons *see Ranunculus*
bamboo 32, 34, 37, 38, 135
bamboo, bush 132
barberry *see Berberis*
basil 187
bear moss (*Polytrichum commune*) 56
bearberry (*Arctostaphylos uva-ursi*) 28
beech *see Fagus*; hedges
    copper 63
Begonia 39, 76, 85
bellflower *see Campanula*
Bellis perennis (daisy) 182
Berberis (barberry) 64, 65, 66, 68, 70, 132
Bergenia (elephant's ears) 56, 75, 166
Beskov, Elsa 156
Betula (birch) 6, 26, 32, 51, 65, 72, 75-7, 92, 95, 147, 150, 163, 166-7, 171, 173, 181
    ermanii 'Mount Apoi' 156, 157
    pendula 163
    utilis var. *jacquemontii* 152, 153, 173
bilberry 6, 28, 58, 75, 156
birch *see Betula*
bishop's mitre (*Epimedium*) 46
bistort *see Persicaria*
Bjärred 42
blackcurrant 48, 51, 182
blackthorn 32
bleeding heart *see Dicentra*
Blixen, Karen 4, 10, 106, 108, 111, 182
Block, Hans Raszmusson 6
bloodroot (*Sanguinaria canadensis*) 139
bluebell, Spanish (*Hyacinthoides hispanica*) 65
blue oat grass *see Helictotrichon sempervirens*
bog moss *see Sphagnum*
Böll, Heinrich 80
Borago officinalis (borage) 22
Börjesson, Maria 132
box *see Buxus*
Brantevik 112-15, 158-61
Bruun, Andreas 108, 147, 148
buckthorn (*Rhamnus*) 65
buckthorn, sea (*Hippophae rhamnoides*) 34
bugloss, viper's (*Echium vulgare*) 112, 114
Bühler, Karl-Dietrich 6
Bull, Schak 120
bulrush *see Typha*
butter burr (*Petasites albus*) 106
Buxus (box) 6, 14, 30, 32-4, 39, 44, 72, 131-2, 140, 142-4, 150, 158, 160-1, 171, 174
Calluna vulgaris (heather) 40
Caltha palustris (marsh marigold) 95
Camassia leichtlinii (quamash) 152
Campanula (bellflower) 139, 160
    alliariifolia 187

carpatica 187
    persicifolia 142, 152, 156
campion, rose (*Lychnis coronaria*) 94, 95, 99
Carex (sedge) 95
    muskingumensis (palm branch sedge) 152
Carlsen, Caroline 106, 110
carnation 22
caryopteris 33
catchfly toadstools 61
catmint (*Nepeta*) 108
cat's ears (*Antennaria*) 152
Centaurea cyanus (cornflower) 182
cherry *see Prunus*
chestnut 62, 92; *see also* horse chestnut
children's gardens 14, 17, 39, 156
Christmas rose (*Helleborus niger*) 46
Cimicifuga racemosa (snake-root) 64, 65, 128
Clematis 22, 46, 70, 132, 134
    alpina 150, 167
    potaninii (syn. *fargesii* var. *souliei*) 131
    macropetala 150
    'Mrs T. Lundell' 152
columbine (*Aquilegia*) 14, 95, 139
coneflower 99, 135
conifers 6, 32, 46, 147
Consolida (larkspur) 22, 51
Convallaria majalis (lily-of-the-valley) 14
Coreopsis verticillata (tickseed) 65
cornelian cherry (*Cornus mas*) 17
cornflower *see Centaurea cyanus*
Cornus 17, 28, 99
    kousa var. *chinensis* 139
    mas (cornelian cherry) 17
Corydalis 95, 152
Cotinus coggygria 132
cow parsley (*Anthriscus sylvestris*) 114
cowslip (*Primula veris*) 152
crab apple *see Malus*
Crambe maritima (sea kale) 114
cranberry 58, 61, 156
cranesbill *see Geranium*
Crataegus (hawthorn) 14, 17, 20-2, 38, 171, 174
    intricata 65
Crocus 65, 128
currants 20, 21, 48, 51, 64, 104, 182
Cyclamen hederifolium 157
Cymbalaria muralis (ivy-leaved toadflax) 16
Dactylorhiza maculata (spotted orchid) 157
daffodil 14, 54, 128
daisy 30, 95, 153, 182, 184
Dalby 152-7
dandelion 30, 32, 38-9, 110, 129
Daphne mezereum (mezereon) 64
daylily (*Hererocallis*) 157
De horticoltura danica 6
decorative objects 148, 158-9, 161, 168
    ceramics 16, 33, 128, 130, 177
    found objects 17-18, 36, 99, 159
    glass 32, 34, 37, 48, 51, 99, 170
    stone 32, 48, 136, 148, 168, 170
    see also sculpture
Degernes, Rakkestad 62-5
Delphinium 21, 102, 134, 167, 184
Dianthus deltoides (maiden pink) 44, 63
    gratianopolitanus 28
Diascia barberae 64
Dicentra 30, 51; *eximia* 102, 104
Dicranum scoparium (moss) 60
dill (*Anethum graveolens*) 21, 22
Dinesen, Wilhelm 108, 111

dock (*Rumex*) 104, 108
dogwood *see Cornus*
Dröm, Johan 54
Dunér, Sten and Katarina 9, 48, 51, 54, 170
Echinacea purpurea (purple coneflower) 135
Echinops (globe thistle) 34, 84, 85
Echium vulgare (viper's bugloss) 112, 114
elder *see Sambucus*
elephant's ears *see Bergenia*
elm *see Ulmus*
Emanuelsson, Helena 9, 92, 94, 99
Emdrup 11
Empetrum nigrum 157
Epilobium (willow herb) 58
Epimedium (bishop's mitre) 46
Eranthis hyemalis 181, 182
Erigeron 'Foerster's Liebling' 143
Euonymus (spindle) 17, 64, 132, 153
Eupatorium purpureum (Joe Pye weed) 65, 135
Euphorbia griffithii 132
everlasting pea (*Lathyrus grandiflorus*) 134
Ewald, Johannes 106, 110, 111
Exochorda serratifolia 156
Fagus (beech) 6, 20-1, 30, 32, 38, 63-4, 88, 90, 108, 118, 126-8, 171, 174, 182
Fahnehjelm, Catharina 92
false acacia 30
false mallow (*Sidalcea*) 95
ferns 28, 32, 36, 42, 75, 116, 119, 135, 157, 166
fescue, blue *see Festuca glauca*
Festuca glauca (blue fescue) 34
Ficus carica (fig) 44, 142, 143
figwort 95
Filipendula ulmaria (meadowsweet) 94, 95, 99
Flade by Limfjord 20-5
flax (*Linum*) 20, 22, 24, 44
Foerster, Karl 143, 181
forget-me-not 14, 34, 99
Forsythia ovata (Korean forsythia) 167
foxglove 33, 51, 56, 73, 99, 148
Frank, Josef 139
Friberg, Per 10, 40, 42
Frölich, Kaare and Torborg 10, 72, 75
Fuchsia 22, 44, 46, 158, 159, 160
Gabrielsen, Egil 9, 76, 80, 83, 84, 85
Gade, Niels W. 120
gardeners' garters (*Phalaris arundinacea* 'Picta') 99
gazebos *see* summer houses
Gentiana sino-ornata (gentian) 64, 157
Geranium (cranesbill) 34, 134, 156
    'Ann Folkard' 139
    dalmaticum 99
    macrorrhizum 26
    psilostemon 134, 139,
    sanguineum 152
    sylvaticum 139
    wallichianum 139
Gesellius, Hermann 10, 163, 178
Geum rivale 95
Gleditsia 32, 39, 132
globe thistle *see Echinops*
goat's rue (*Galega officinalis*) 134
gooseberry 20, 21, 51, 64, 142
grape hyacinths *see Muscari*
grass 20, 22, 24, 28, 34, 42, 56, 76, 99, 104, 136, 139
greenhouses 20, 22, 44, 53, 76, 92, 187
Grieg, Edvard and Nina 10, 11, 72, 75, 116, 119-

122
Grieg, Joachim 122
Grindal, Torsten 187
Gullichsen, Harry and Maire 66, 67, 70
Gustavsson, Eva and Roland 152
Gypsophila 22
Hägle, Harriet 187
Hakonechloa macra 139
Halesia carolina (snowdrop tree) 152
Hamamelis japonica 156
Hamann, Liselotte 88
Hammenhög 170, 177
Hansen, Sven 20
Hansson, Eva and Bertil 130-2, 139
Have, Junggreen 174
hawkweed 28, 56
hawthorn *see Crataegus*
heartsease (*Viola tricolor*) 61
heather 40, 58, 75, 104, 157
Hedeberga 9
hedges 16, 22, 30, 48, 51, 62, 64, 139, 171, 176
    beech 20-23, 32, 38, 88, 90-1, 126-8
    box 140, 144
    hawthorn 14, 17, 38
    hornbeam 108, 130, 135-6, 152, 156
    whitethorn 106
    willow 162, 163
    yew 21, 46, 130, 132, 134, 136, 174
Heide, Erik 20, 22, 24
Helianthus salicifolius 34
Helictotrichon sempervirens 34, 134
Helleborus niger (Christmas rose) 46
Helsinki 162-7
Hemerocallis (daylily) 153, 156, 157
Hemgård, Gretel 10, 163
Hepatica nobilis 182
Heracleum (tromsøpalme) 76, 77, 83, 85
herbs 6, 20, 32, 51, 99
Herning 11, 176
Hertel, Lisbeth 110
Heuchera 132
Hidcote 130, 132
Hieracium (hawkweed) 28, 56
Hippophae rhamnoides (sea buckthorn) 34
Hippuris vulgaris (mare's tail) 37
holly *see Ilex*
Holm, Aase 106
Holte 124-9
honesty (*Lunaria*) 110
honeysuckle *see Lonicera*
hop *see Humulus lupulus*
Hop, Bergen 116-23
hornbeam 108, 130, 135, 136, 152, 156
horse chestnut 64, 80, 83, 99, 102, 106
horseradish 51
Hortus conclusus 6
Hosta (plantain lily) 99, 136, 139, 156
houseleek (*Sempervivum*) 39
Huigens, Dick 32
Humulus lupulus (hop) 32, 53, 64, 65, 71
Hvitträsk 10, 163, 170, 178
hyacinth 65
Hyacinthoides hispanica (Spanish bluebell) 65
Hydrangea 18, 32, 152, 167
    arborescens 158
    paniculata 99, 158, 160
    anomala subsp. *petiolaris* 18, 68, 130, 131
Ilex (holly) 72, 99; *aquifolium* 131
Impatiens 94
Indian mallow (*Abutilon*) 44

Inula ensifolia 128
Iris 51, 145, 152, 166
    'Joanna Taylor' 152
    'Maori King' 152
    pseudocorus 37, 152
    sibirica 145, 166
Irvine, Simon 177
ivy 6, 14, 39, 46, 99, 127, 128, 132
ivy-leaved toadflax (Cymbalaria muralis) 16
Jansson, Tove 58
Japanese gardens 60-1, 130, 135-6, 166-7, 170
Japanese maple see Acer
Japanese pagoda tree (Sophora japonica) 30
Japanese painted fern see Athyrium niponicum
jasmine 88
Jerusalem cross (Lychnis chalcedonica) 95
Johnson, Barbara 44
Jonsson, Henrik 92
juneberry (Amelanchier spicata) 65, 156
Juniperus 72, 75, 148
Kihlman, Botvid 44
Kirengeshoma palmata 136
Klingborg, Arne 187
Knautia macedonica 134
Køge 147-51
Koldinghus 6
Kraitz, Gustav 16
laburnum 147, 148
lady's mantle see Alchemilla mollis
Lagerlöf, Selma 9, 44
lamb's ears (Stachys byzantina) 95, 110
Lamium galeobdolon 75
Långedrag 9, 100-5
larkspur (Consolida) 22, 51
Lathyrus 20, 21, 22, 158; grandiflora 134
Lavatera (mallow) 20, 22, 134
lavender 14, 20-1, 44, 46, 108, 140, 142-3
Leptinella minor (syn. Cotula minor) 152
Leucanthemum vulgare 66, 182, 184
Leucobryum glaucum (pin-cushion moss) 60
Leucojum vernum (snowflake) 106, 108, 181
Li, Grethe and Olav 26, 28
lichen 56, 58, 61, 116
Lidingö 9, 44
Ligularia 63, 77, 85
    'The Rocket' 76
Ligustrum (privet) 6, 14, 18, 32, 171, 174
lilac, common see Syringa vulgaris
Lilium (lily) 64, 76, 77, 184
    'Apeldoorn' 95
    candidum (Madonna lily) 46, 161
    martagon 17, 28
lily, African see Agapanthus
lily-of-the-valley (Convallaria majalis) 14
lilyturf, black dragon see Ophiopogon
lime 62, 64, 65, 110, 171
Linaria (toad flax) 134
Lindgren, Armas 10, 163, 178
Linnaea borealis (twin-flower) 157
Linné, Carl von (Linnaeus) 157, 182
Linum (flax) 44
Ljunghusen 10, 40-3
Lobelia 131
Loegum Kloster 174
Lonicera (honeysuckle) 40
    caerulea 65
    caprifolium 42, 166, 167
    henryi 140, 150
    involucrata 65

periclymenum 64
prolifera 134
Lørenskog 26-9
Lötveit, Eilif B. 116
Lunaria (honesty) 110
Lund 9, 130-9
Lundberg, Emma 44
Lundberg, Håkan 100
Lundström, Helge 112, 114
lupins 51
Lychnis chalcedonica (Jerusalem Cross) 51, 95
    coronaria 94, 95
Lysimachia (loosestrife)
    nummularia 139
    punctata 76-7, 85, 99
    vulgaris 95
Lythrum 51, 53, 135; salicaria 95
Macleaya cordata (plume poppy) 167
magnolia 152
Mahonia aquifolium 17, 65, 159
maiden grass see Miscanthus sinensis
maiden pink see Dianthus deltoides
mallow see Lavatera
Malmö castle park 114
Malus baccata 65; sargentii 91; see also apple
maple see Acer
mare's tail (Hippuris vulgaris) 37
marguerite 66, 67, 95, 143, 158
marigold 76, 77, 81, 85
marjoram (Origanum) 99
marram grass (Ammophila arenaria) 114
marsh ledum (Ledum palustre) 38, 157
marsh marigold (Caltha palustris) 95
masterwort see Astrantia
Matteuccia struthiopteris (ostrich fern) 166
meadow buttercup (Ranunculus acris) 95
meadow rue (Thalictrum aquilegiifolium) 26
meadowsweet (Filipendula ulmaria) 94, 95, 99
Meconopsis cambrica (Welsh poppy) 139
mezereon (Daphne mezereum) 64
milkweed see Euphorbia
Milles, Carl 9, 171, 173
Millesgården 173, 181
mirabelle plum 32, 33
Miscanthus sinensis 39; 'Gracillimus' 34, 156
Mochizuki, Akira 170, 171
mock orange see Philadelphus
Mohr, Aslaug 122
Mölandet 10, 56-61
monkey puzzle (Araucaria araucana) 160
monkshood see Aconitum napellus)
Morus nigra (mulberry) 143
Moscheles, Ignaz 121
moss 28, 56, 58, 99, 156, 166-7; gardens 60-1
mountain ash see Sorbus
mugo pine 174
mugwort see Artemisia; Seriphidium
mulberry (Morus nigra) 143
mullein (Verbascum) 63
Muscari (grape hyacinth) 65, 128
Muuratsalo 10, 170
Myrica gale (sweet gale) 157
Naerum 11, 129, 176
Narcissus poeticus 143
Näs 9, 92
Nemophila menziesii (baby blue-eyes) 99
Nepeta x fasenii (catmint) 108
Nesttun 72-5
nettles 65, 94
New Zealand burr see Acaena

Nilsson, Kjell 112
Noormarkku 10, 66-71
Nordborg, Jan-Erik 187
Nordström, Thomas 4, 140, 142, 143, 145, 178
Norway spruce (Picea abies) 99
Novalis 9, 48
Nymphaea (waterlily) 34, 46, 84, 85
oak see Quercus
oat grass see Helictotrichon
Oenothera (sundrop) 62, 63
oleander 22
Omphalodes verna 143
Ophiopogon planiscapus 'Nigrescens' 136
orchid, spotted (Dactylorhiza maculata) 157
Oregon grape (Mahonia aquifolium) 17, 65, 159
Origanum (marjoram) 99
orpine (Sedum telephium) 135
osier, purple (Salix purpurea) 162
Oskarson, Annika 178
Osmunda 153, 156, 157
Österlen 181
ostrich fern (Matteuccia struthiopteris) 166
Oxalis corniculata (shamrock) 27, 28
oxeye daisy (Leucanthemum vulgare) 30, 95
Paeonia (peony) 28, 51, 65,
    lactiflora 143, 145
pansy 56, 64
Papaver (poppy) 182
    alpinum 27-8
    nudicaule 147
    orientale 95
    rhoeas 112
    somniferum 108
parsley (Petroselinum crispum) 22
Parthenocissus inserta 66, 68
pear 46, 104, 171
Pelargonium 44, 184
peony 28, 51, 65, 143, 145
periwinkle (Vinca minor) 39
Persicaria (bistort) 95, 135
Petasites albus (butter burr) 106, 182
Petroselinum crispum (parsley) 22
Phalaris arundinacea 'Picta' 99
Philadelphus (mock orange) 63, 64, 132
Philodendron cordatum 68, 71
Phlox 65, 134
Phyllostachys aurea (fishpole bamboo) 34
Picea abies (Norway spruce) 99
Pilosella aurantiaca (hawkweed) 56
pin-cushion moss (Leucobryum glaucum) 60
pine 26, 40, 65, 67, 140, 157, 166
Pinus sylvestris (Scots pine) 157
plane 140, 143, 144
plantain lily see Hosta
play areas 39, 88, 90, 112, 129
Pleioblastus auricomus (bush bamboo) 132
plume poppy (Macleaya cordata) 167
Poll, Sonja 11, 126, 128
Polypodium vulgare (common polypody) 61
Polytrichum 56, 58, 60, 61
poppy see Papaver
potato 24, 51
potato bush see Solanum rantonnetii
Poulsen nurseries 108
primrose 108
Primula 14, 95, 152
privet see Ligustrum
Prunus 46, 75, 90, 91, 104, 164, 171
    avium 152
    laurocerasus (cherry laurel) 99, 129

maackii 152
padus 38
pensylvanica 166
tenella (Russian almond) 166
Pulmonaria 143
pumpkin 160
purple loosestrife see Lythrum
quamash (Camassia) 152
Quercus (oak) 32, 38, 39, 40, 65, 126, 128, 171
    robur (common oak) 22, 65
Ranunculus 65, 95
raspberry 6, 182
    flowering (Rubus odoratus) 51, 167
redcurrant 20, 48, 51, 104
reed 88, 94, 99
Rhamnus frangula (alder buckthorn) 65
Rheum palmatum (Chinese rhubarb) 36
Rhododendron 26, 66, 72, 75, 116, 119, 147-8, 152, 171, 181
    canadense 157
    'Catawbiense grandiflorum' 148
    hirsutum 28
    yakushimanum 38
rhubarb, Chinese (Rheum palmatum) 36
Richter, Bruno 178
Robinia 150
Rodgersia 37, 135, 166
Ronneby park 170, 171
Rosa (rose) 17, 21-2, 44, 92, 99, 103, 158-9, 168; bush 30, 32, 39, 46, 56; climbing 20, 46, 184
    'Golden Showers' 30; 'Gruss an Aachen' 106; 'Karen Blixen' 108; 'Iceberg' 33; 'Kiftsgate' 187; 'New Dawn' 140, 142, 152; Polyantha 106; 'Schneewittchen' 33; 'Sympathie' 104
    R. canina 181
    R. glauca (syn. R. rubrifolia) 134, 135
    R. pimpinellifolia 34
    R. rugosa 51
Rosendal Barony, Norway 6, 168
Rosendal Park, Stockholm 173, 178
rowan 26, 40
royal fern (Osmunda regalis) 157
Rubus odoratus (flowering raspberry) 51, 167
Rudbeckia laciniata (coneflower) 99
Rudolf Steiner Seminar (College) 178, 187
Rumex (dock) 104
Rungstedlund 10, 106-11
rush (Schoenoplectus lacustris) 152
Saarinen, Eliel 10, 163, 178
sage see Salvia
Salix (willow) 14, 32, 37-8, 64-5, 70, 91, 99
    alba 38; a. var. sericea 66, 68, 171
    exigua 34, 39
    hastata 38, 157
    helvetica 30, 132
    koriyanagi 153
    purpurea 'Nana' 64, 162, 163
Salminen, Pekka 10, 162, 163, 166
Salto, Lulu 187
Salvia (sage)
    'Mainacht' 139
    nemerosa 134
    officinalis 142
Sambucus racemosa (elder) 104, 132
Sanguinaria canadensis (bloodroot) 139
Saponaria officinalis (soapwort) 16
Saxifraga (saxifrage) 27-8, 153, 166, 167
Scaevola saligna 64
Schoenoplectus lacustris (rush) 152

Schønherr, Torben 88, 90, 91, 174
Scilla (squill) 65
Scots pine (Pinus sylvestris) 157
screens 132, 135-6, 140, 173, 178
sculpture 16, 20-2, 24, 39, 68, 73, 85, 114, 170-1, 173-4, 177, 181; animal 9, 76-7, 80-84, 131-2, 158; cloth 140, 143, 144; statues 122, 150, 159, 160; tree 14, 36, 38, 42, 166; see also topiary
sea kale (Crambe maritima) 114
sedge see Carex
Sedum 28, 34, 61, 63, 99, 102, 104, 135
Sempervivum (houseleek) 39, 104
Seriphidium maritimum (syn. Artemisia maritima, mugwort) 114
serviceberry, Allegheny see Amelanchier
shadbush (Amelanchier canadensis) 64
shamrock (Oxalis corniculata) 27, 28
Sidalcea (false mallow) 94, 95
Silkeborg 86-91, 88, 88-91
silver birch see Betula pendula
Simons, Tom and Maj 10, 56, 61
Simrishamn 140-6
Skaarer, Nils and Sigrid 62, 65
snake-bark maple see Acer
snake-root (Cimicifuga racemosa) 64, 65, 128
snowball tree (Viburnum opulus) 62
snowberry (Symphoricarpos) 17, 38, 54, 65
snowdrop 181
snowdrop tree (Halesia carolina) 152
snowflake, summer see Leucojum aestivum

soapwort see Saponaria officinalis
Södra Sandby 14-19
Solanum rantonnetii (blue potato bush) 65
Søndre Finstad 76-85
Sophora japonica 32
Sorbus (mountain ash, rowan, whitebeam) 6, 21, 30, 32, 39, 77, 83, 106, 111, 116, 135, 171
    americana 130
    aucuparia 42,
    koehneana 139
Sørensen, C.Th. 11, 126, 129, 174, 176, 177
Sørensen, Henning 88
Spartina pectinata 34
speedwell (Veronica) 56, 114
Sphagnum (moss) 58, 60, 61, 156
spindle see Euonymus
Spiraea 51, 64, 99, 166
Spodiopogon sibiricus 152
squill (Scilla) 65
Stachys byzantina (lamb's ears) 95, 110
Stenberg, Brigitta 177
strawberry 20-2, 39, 127, 128
sundrop (Oenothera) 62, 63
sweet gale (Myrica gale) 157
sweet pea see Lathyrus
sycamore see Acer pseudoplatanus
Symphoricarpos (snowberry) 17, 38, 65
Syringa vulgaris 30, 48, 56, 64, 76, 174
Tagetes (marigold) 76
tallvitmossa (Sphagnum nemorcum) 58
Taraxacum officinale 182

Taxus (yew) 6, 20-1, 30, 34, 46, 61, 72, 130, 132, 134, 136, 150, 171, 174
Thalictrum aquilegiifolium (meadow rue) 26
thrift, sea (Armeria maritima) 65, 112, 114
thyme 34, 148, 152, 166
tickseed (Coreopsis verticillata) 65
toadflax (Linaria) 134
tomato 44, 187
Tomelilla 9, 30-9
Tomarps Gård 177
topiary 51, 143, 168, 174
    box 130-2, 144, 159, 160-1; hawthorn 9, 14, 20-1; privet 14
Tradescantia x andersoniana 142, 143
Tranås 9, 92-9
Trillium 65, 157
trinity flower (Trillium) 65
Troldhaugen 10, 72, 75, 116-23
tromsøpalme (Heracleum) 83
Tsuga canadensis 148
tulip 14, 65, 110, 132, 152
twin-flower (Linnaea borealis) 157
twinberry (Lonicera involucrata) 65
Typha (bulrush) 38, 152
Ulmus (elm) 30, 32, 39, 135-6, 171
Vaccinium 156
Vancouveria hexandra 153
Värnamo 9, 48-55
Verbascum (mullein) 63, 95
Verbena 134
Veronica (speedwell) 56, 114

Veronicastrum virginicum 94, 95
Viburnum 62, 64, 145, 150
Vik, Ingebrigt 122
Villa Mairea 10, 66-71
Vinca minor (lesser periwinkle) 39, 166
Viola 22, 30, 61, 95, 108, 184
violet see Viola
Viotti, Ulla 177, 181
Waldsteinia ternata 150, 166
walnut 143
Wassberg, Karin 159, 161
water plaintain (Alisma) 38
water-lily see Nymphaea
Welsh poppy (Meconopsis cambrica) 139
Wennerlund, Alfred 100
Werenskiold, Erik 116, 122
whitecurrant 51
whitethorn (Crataegus) 22, 106, 174
Wiese, Otto 173
wild chervil 110
wild garlic (Allium ursinum) 14
wild ginger see Asarum
willow see Salix
willow herb (Epilobium) 58
Wisteria 44, 46, 140, 142-3, 148
Wohlert, Vilhelm 108
wood anemone (Anemone nemerosa) 152
wood lily (Trillium) 157
yew see Taxus
Ytterjärna 178, 187
Zantedeschia (arum lily) 22

Author's Acknowledgments

I am indebted to Frances Lincoln for believing in my book from the start and then turning it into reality with her highly professional staff. The cooperation with Jo Christian, Alison Freegard and Caroline Hillier has been most agreeable and enjoyable and I would like to express my heartfelt gratitude to them for this. Likewise I would like to thank John Margetts most warmly for his sensitive English translation of my German text.

I would like to thank Christian Eilers for permission to quote extensively from *Karen Blixen's Flowers*, published by his publishing house, and acknowledgment is also due to the authors of the various chapters from which I have quoted: Sven-Ingvar Andersson, Lisbeth Hertel and the late Steen Eiler Rasmussen.

I owe particular thanks to the following garden owners for permission to photograph their gardens for the book, and to those who have readily given me their help and advice: Sven-Ingvar Andersson, Marianne Wirenfeldt Asmussen, Elsie and Yngve Bernhardsson, Andreas Bruun, Katarina and Sten Dunér, Mette Eggen, Helena and Gunnar Emanuelsson, Madeleine von Essen, Per Friberg, Torborg and Kaare Frölich, Solveig Gabrielsen, Susanne Guldager, Eva and Roland Gustavsson, Anna Hall, Liselotte Hamann, Eva and Bertil Hansson, Erik Heide, Gretel Hemgård, Bente Hjelmar, Aase Holm, Simon Irvine, Barbara Johnson, David Kallos, Jürgen Kellerhoff, Botvid Kihlman, Päivi and Pekka Kuokka, Grethe and Olav Li, Kråke Lithander, Eilif B. Lötveit, Annemarie Lund, Håkan Lundberg, Helge Lundström, Ulrich Neuhaus, Irmgard Nickel, Tommy Nordström, Sonja Poll, Bruno Richter, Pekka and Jarkko Salminen, Gösta and Kerstin Sandlund, Maj and Tom Simons, Solveig Stenholm, Lulu Salto Stephensen, Torben Schønherr, Nils and Sigrid Skaarer, Henning Sørensen, Karin Wassberg, William Wareing and Otto Wiese.

Finally I would like to thank the staff of the following gardens and museums for their helpful and ever ready cooperation whenever I had questions: Alvar Aalto Museum, Jyväskylä, Finland; the Karen Blixen Museum, Rungstedlund, Denmark; Edvard Grieg Museum-Troldhaugen, Bergen, Norway; Mairea Foundation, Noormarkku, Finland; Millesgården, Lidingö, Sweden; Rosendals Trädgård (Garden), Stockholm; Rudolf Steiner Seminar (College), Ytterjärna, Sweden; Emil Wikström Museum, Visavuori, Valkeakoski, Finland (*pavilion shown opposite*); and the Hvitträsk Museum, Kirkkonumi, Finland.

Publishers' Acknowledgments

Frances Lincoln Publishers would like to thank the following for their help in producing this book: Graham Gosling for translating Milena Matteini's Italian texts; Alison Barratt for additional drawings of garden plans; Roger Hillier and Sarah Pickering for design assistance; Pat Farrington for proof reading, and Elizabeth Wiggans for the index.

Project editor Alison Freegard   Editorial Director Kate Cave
Commissioning editor Jo Christian   Production Hazel Kirkman
Art Direction & Design Caroline Hillier   Horticultural Consultant Tony Lord